ALL GIRL
scrapbook pages

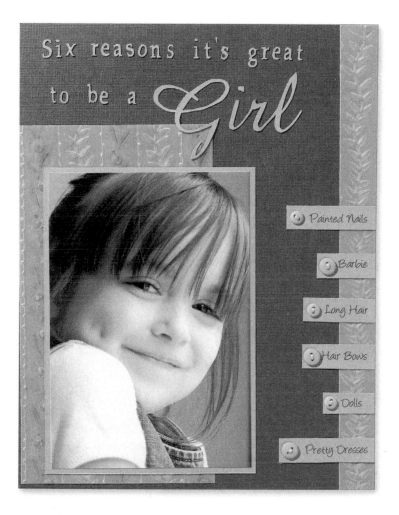

Six reasons it's great to be a Girl

- Painted Nails
- Barbie
- Long Hair
- Hair Bows
- Dolls
- Pretty Dresses

the growing up years

MEMORY
MAKERS
BOOKS

Executive Editor Kerry Arquette   *Founder* Michele Gerbrandt

Editor Emily Curry Hitchingham

Art Director Andrea Zocchi

Designer Nick Nyffeler

Art Acquisitions Editor Janetta Abucejo Wieneke

Craft Editor Jodi Amidei

Photographer Ken Trujillo

Contributing Photographers Brenda Martinez, Jennifer Reeves

Contributing Designer Karen Roehl

Art Caption Writer Brandi Ginn

Contributing Artists See Artist Index on page 110

Editorial Support Dena Twinem, MaryJo Regier, Karen Cain

Memory Makers® All Girl Scrapbook Pages

Published by Memory Makers Books, an imprint of F&W Publications, Inc.

12365 Huron Street, Suite 500, Denver, CO 80234

Phone 1-800-254-9124

First edition. Printed in the United States of America.

08 07 06 05 04 5 4 3 2

A catalog record for this book is available from the U.S. Library of Congress

Distributed to trade and art markets by

F&W Publications, Inc.

4700 East Galbraith Road, Cincinnati, OH 45236

Phone 1-800-289-0963

ISBN 1-892127-35-0

Memory Makers Books is the home of *Memory Makers*, the scrapbook magazine dedicated to educating and inspiring scrapbookers. To subscribe, or for more information, call 1-800-366-6465.
Visit us on the Internet at www.memorymakersmagazine.com.

This book belongs to

_____

We dedicate this book to all of our contributors
who graciously shared their endearing girl scrapbook pages with
us and who may now be even more inspired to preserve
cherished girlhood memories.

Table Of Contents

 **one**

8-33 Sugar and...

46 endearing page ideas featuring the inherent charm of girls—from their sweet smiles and tenderhearted dispositions to moments of quiet contemplation and curious discoveries

two

34-59 Spice!

42 innovative page ideas for celebrating the irresistible spirit of girls—from out-there antics and all-that attitudes to silly expressions and spunky self-determination

three

four

Introduction

Just what is it about girls that enables them to so effortlessly wrap us around their little fingers? Is it the giggles in their voices and secrets in their smiles, or the way they bounce between silliness and sophistication, precociousness and preciousness? While we wonder at the inherent charm of girls, they grow from children to young women and redefine the word "endearing" all over again. The growing- up years are exciting and eventful times that girls and those who love them should cherish. To be a girl, to raise a girl, or to love a girl is a wonderful gift of fate.

As a mother of two daughters, I am reminded every day just how special, unique and sometimes challenging girls are. A wonderful aspect about being a mother, aunt or grandmother to a young girl is that you inevitably return to your own girlhood through her experiences. For instance, do you remember all those sleepless slumber parties and times spent playing with your Barbie dolls? The anticipation of getting your ears pierced? How about the exhilarating freedom of your first excursion to the local mall or movie theater without a parental chaperone? I'll bet you have stories about getting into your mother's make-up, trying out new hairstyles and countless hours of playing make-believe and dress-up. High school dances. Team sports. Dreams of travel. Best girlfriends and the next boyfriend. With each generation there are shared experiences between women and girls that will remain defining moments. And just as surely, there'll be times when we'll think we were never so sophisticated, independent, and poised for success as young girls are today.

All Girl Scrapbook Pages is intended to help you capture and celebrate the "sugar and spice" of the special girl in your life. Whether she is a rough n' tumble ballplayer or a prima ballerina, a fashion diva-in-the-making or a fan of dirty faces and grass stains, you're sure to find inspiration in the hearwarming and all-around wonderful layouts featured. You'll also discover tips for compiling lasting scrapbook albums as well as outstanding page title ideas.

In a flash, little girls become little women. Therefore it is important to capture their silly expressions, curious discoveries, zany statements, astounding milestones and unsuspecting moments as they unfold. In doing so you preserve all of their precious qualities and treasured times in your scrapbooks to revisit in years to come.

Michele

Michele Gerbrandt
Founding Editor
Memory Makers magazine

Supplies For Making Lasting Albums

The use of high-quality scrapbook materials will ensure your cherished girlhood memories stay the course of time. We recommend the following:

- Archival-quality albums

- PVC-free page protectors

- Acid- and lignin-free papers

- Acid-free and photo-safe adhesives

- Pigment-ink pens and markers

- PVC-free memorabilia keepers, sleeves or envelopes

- Flat, photo-safe embellishments (encapsulate or place away from photos if questionable)

- De-acidifying spray for news clippings or documents

How To Make A Scrapbook Page

BUILDING A PAGE FROM THE BACKGROUND OUT

Start with a selection of one to five photos for a single page and gather any appropriate memorabilia. Select a background paper that pulls one color from your photos. You may wish to choose additional papers, also based on colors found in photos. Pick out or make page additions that complement photos, if desired. Loosely assemble photos, title, journaling, memorabilia and page accents to form a visually appealing layout. Trim and mat photos, then mount in place with adhesive. Add title and journaling. Complete page with any additional accents. For instructions on how to replicate this page exactly, see page 109.

Sugar and...

The old adage about what little girls are made of still holds unfailingly true. Sugar is sweet and so too are young girls. Embodying all that is exceptionally nice, girls seem to innately possess tender hearts and sensitive souls. Girls are the bearers of bountiful smiles, warm hugs and contagious laughter. It's this sweet side of a girl's personality that prompts those moments that melt your heart and lift your spirits. Lovely and loving, the charm of young girls is both plain to see and beyond skin-deep. Maybe it's in their animated faces and endearing giggles. Maybe it's in their dreamy demeanor and delight in newfound discoveries. Perhaps it's in their whirly carefree ways of play or that girls are simply chock-full of big dreams and wondrous wishes. No matter what form it takes, the sweet nature of young girls is like the countenance of angels: unspoiled, unspoken and unquestionably pure of heart.

Mercedes, 5

Parris, 3

Little girls are the nicest things that happen to people. They are born with a little bit of angelshine about them...

—*Alan Beck*

Little Girls Like Butterflies Need No Excuse

Mary Anne used feminine detail to create the delicate handcrafted border that frames her layout. Print mirror image of font along each side of pink cardstock. Cut with a craft knife, leaving tops and bottoms intact; remove center to form border. Create butterfly in border by using embossed vellum buterfly as a guide and cutting with a craft knife. Using border punch (Fiskars), create floral outer edge. Adhere border to dark pink background. Triple mat photo on dark and light pink papers and adhere to page. Print journaling onto vellum; adhere to page with spray adhesive and accent with embossed vellum butterflies (K & Company).

Mary Anne Walters, Hampshire, England

Wonder

Jodi added dimension and visual interest by framing photos inside shadowboxes. Use a craft knife to cut windows in foam core where photos will appear; adhere photos to foam core so that photos are revealed. Also using a craft knife, cut slightly smaller windows in same positions from a 12 x 12" piece of dark pink textured cardstock (Bazzill) so that foam core beneath is concealed. Mount to foam core. Cut strips of burgundy paper with mitered corners to frame "windows." Add blocks of specialty paper (Pulsar) with chalked edges for embellishments and journaling block; adorn decorative blocks with silk flowers and leaves (Pulsar). Use lettering template (Provo Craft) for title; chalk edges to complete.

Jodi Amidei, Memory Makers Books

The Walking Umbrella

Diana's color choices and page accents were inspired by her daughter's charming raincoat and umbrella. Begin with pink and yellow gingham paper (Close To My Heart) for various background blocks; accent with eyelets, metal flower (Making Memories), button (Making Memories), and green rickrack. Layer with punched flower shapes and additional buttons. Use mesh paper (Magenta) for two of the remaining backgrounds. Place additional buttons (Jo Ann Fabrics) on one piece; embellish the other with square vellum tags layered with ABC stickers (Provo Craft), flower eyelets (Stamp Doctor), buttons (Making Memories), and embroidery floss (DMC). Gently rub pink paper with a fine-grit sandpaper. Journal poem and title; cut tag shape and journaling block from pink sanded paper. Complete page by adorning tag with additional eyelets, buttons and embroidery floss.

Diana Graham, Barrington, Illinois

Always Remember to Be Happy

Amy used a quote as both a unique page accent and to capture the essence of joy in her niece, Michelle. Re-create this computer generated layout (Adobe Photoshop 6.0) using filter and sketch options. Create rectangular box; color and fill with text. Draw intersecting lines using the pencil tool. Resize original photo and add as a new layer. To manually re-create this layout, enlarge photo and trace image with pink chalk pencils. Print journaling quote on pink paper; cut and mount on traced image. Adhere reduced image of original photo over traced image.

Amy Alvis, Indianapolis, Indiana

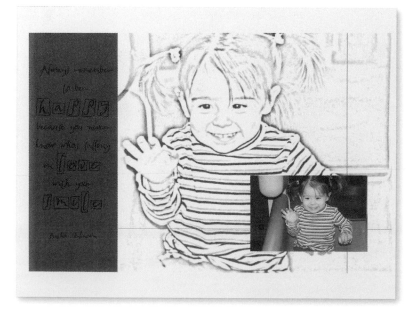

Kisses

Diana combined feminine accents, soft colors and decorated vellum tags to complement these sweet pictures of her daughter. Frame one photo on pink cardstock; slightly tear and roll edges and adhere to page. Mount two pictures directly onto pink patterned paper (Creative Imaginations). Create title by layering letter stickers (Creative Imaginations) on vellum tags (Making Memories); adhere with foam adhesive. Print journaling onto vellum (Close To My Heart) and attach with snaps (Chatterbox). Accent with kiss stamp (Close To My Heart) and date stamp (Making Memories) applied to vellum tag (Making Memories). Layer with metal letter (Making Memories) and finish with fiber.

Diana Graham, Barrington, Illinois

All You Need To Be Is You...

Martha chose vibrant colors and multiple patterns to create a cheerful and whimsical page. Double mat photo with pink textured cardstock (Bazzill) and green paper. Mount on patterned paper (KI Memories). Print journaling on a transparency and layer on striped paper (KI Memories); mount to page to create border along left side. Construct embellishment by decorating a gift bag (Hallmark) with jewels (Scrapyard 329). Layer tag with poem stone (Creative Imaginations) and pink and orange fibers.

Martha Crowther, Salem, New Hampshire
Photo: Cristina Arroyo, Falucho, La Mirada, California

Sweet Sisters

Melissa created texture in her page by combining several three-dimensional techniques. To create patterned paper, tear sheets of colored tissue paper and adhere with decoupage adhesive. When dry, paint with lumiere paints (Jacquard). Create tree branches by rolling pieces of aluminum foil; layer with paper towels and apply gesso (Liquitex). When dry, apply brown paint. Age fairies (www.paperphernalia.com) with sandpaper and adhere with decoupage adhesive. Cut aluminum foil leaves by hand; paint, allow to dry and use to accent branches. Embellish with page corners made from paper clay painted with lumiere paint, and folded-over copper sheets (AMACO). Print journaling onto transparency (3M) using colored ink. Print title on transparency; set with gold embossing powder.

Melissa Smith, Jacksonville, North Carolina

Believe, Hope, Dream

With its artful design and eye-appealing composition, who would guess that Melissa's layout is comprised of less-than-perfect photos? Here strategic photo cropping and paper layering conceal imperfections to create a striking page. Cut strips of green patterned paper (Anna Griffin); affix along the bottom third and right side of page. Using a craft knife, cut two slits in patterned paper for picture to slide into. Tear another piece of green patterned paper, place in upper left corner and layer pictures on top. Punch squares from patterned paper and affix to bottom of page with eyelets; accent with metal word charms (Making Memories). Complete page by embellishing patterned paper strip with metal heart charms (Making Memories) affixed with eyelets.

Melissa Brown, Fort Walton Beach, Florida

Snapshots of Spring

Barb captured her daughter in the midst of springtime discovery with these striking photos. Create left page by starting with floral patterned paper background (K & Company). Accent flower design with crystal effects (Stampin' Up!) and glass beads. Tear purple textured paper (Bazzill) along the bottom; layer with crumpled green cardstock and photo double-matted on pink cardstocks. Embellish with butterfly die cuts (K & Company) treated with crystal effects, vellum tag (Making Memories) and fibers. Construct right page starting with embossed patterned paper (K & Company). Layer with torn pieces of purple and green cardstocks; accent with vellum tag and embellished die cut adorned with fibers. Print journaling and title onto vellum and adhere.

Barb Hogan, Cincinnati, Ohio

Do You Ever...

As her daughter grows older, Mellette wants her to remember what makes life important. Here a touching poem and picture-perfect composition combine to make for a lovely tribute. Tear floral patterned paper (Dena Designs) and pink cardstock along one edge; layer on green textured paper (Bazzill). Carefully poke evenly spaced holes in green paper along edge of pink cardstock. Poke corresponding holes along edge of patterned paper so that when stitched with embroidery floss (DMC), a zigzag pattern be formed. Print journaling onto vellum; tear along edge. Adhere atop patterned paper with eyelets and embellish with ribbon. Use a complementary photo within a metal frame (Making Memories) to accent border. Repeat tearing and layering technique with main photo mat. Embellish with metal buttons and ribbon to complete.

Mellette Berezoski, Crosby, Texas

True Beauty Comes From Within

Sometimes a striking picture and simple sentiment are all it takes. Make a similar minimalistic layout by tearing embossed vellum (Club Scrap) and layering it atop patterned paper (Club Scrap). Decorate tags (Avery) by first stamping image (Club Scrap) and then washing with complementary ink. String fibers through tags; position beneath photo and adhere to back of page. Mat photo on cardstock and again on linen fabric (Wichelt); mount to patterned paper. Use pen to record journaling.

Ari Macias, Staten Island, New York

Beauty, Innocence

By layering heritage-themed papers and embellishing with old details, Janett accomplished a lovely vintage look. Cut strips of different patterned papers (Anna Griffin, Daisy D's, Karen Foster Design, K & Company) and layer to create background pages. Mount photos to pages; frame bottoms and two sides of pages with tulle and rosette (source unknown) border. Print journaling on vellum; tear along all sides and chalk and ink edges. Create title using ABC stamps (Hero Arts) and gold embossing powder on clear vellum; accent with flower punch art. Embellish with charms (Scrap Arts).

Janett McKee, Austin, Texas

The Kiss

Tammy captured this kiss between her twin girls and enhanced the tender moment with a delicate flower border. Begin with floral patterned paper (Amscan) matted on a black cardstock background. Create dimensional flowers by tearing various sized circles out of pink, lilac and peach cardstocks; chalk and roll edges before layering and adorning with purple rhinestone centers. Adhere purple ribbon (Offray) across top of page. Affix flowers along sides of floral patterned paper and across purple ribbon. Mount photos on lilac mulberry paper (Pulsar), then lilac cardstock. Connect photos and "hang" from purple button by threading wire through eyelets and coiling ends (Making Memories). Complete page by journaling title on torn and chalked lilac cardstock.

Tammy De La Garza, Racine, Wisconsin

A Serious Mood

Although Lauren was excited to lose her tooth, a serious mood came over her thinking the tooth fairy wouldn't be able to find her house. Tear a section diagonally out of embossed green paper (K & Company) and layer on plaid paper (K & Company). Print journaling onto vellum; tear along one side and attach to torn embossed paper with brads. Create title by printing "A" and "mood" on rose-colored cardstock and placing behind vellum title printed with "Serious." Double mat photo on rose and cream-colored papers and place off-center on page. Use chenille rickrack (Offray) for border; accent with crumpled tag adorned with silk leaves, wire, flower beads, and journaling on vellum affixed with brads.

Polly McMillan, Bullhead City, Arizona

Sleep Little Angel

Laura was finally able to get some rest when her two-week-old baby reached exhaustion. Re-create this computer-generated page (Adobe Photoshop 7.0) by creating frames, filling with gray and adding a beveled edge. Use the custom tool to draw moons and stars. Make clouds using the lasso tool; set the feather to 30 pixels. Create metal tags by filling with pink; adjust the opacity to 34 percent and add letters and blending options to create an embossed look. To re-create this page manually, triple mat photos on pink, green, and blue cardstocks. Mount on green paper. Tear and chalk edges of blue vellum to resemble clouds. Layer with metal-rimmed tags strung through fiber. Print title on pink cardstock, tear along bottom edge and adhere to the top of the page. Frame smaller pictures and hang from coiled wire.

Laura Vanderbeek, Logan, Utah
Photos: Tyler Vanderbeek, Logan, Utah

Little Details

Amy captures the precious details of her newborn niece the first time she saw her. Re-create this computer-generated page (Adobe Photoshop 6.0) by adjusting the hue and saturation of a color photo to create a black-and-white image. Add the look of vellum by inserting a new layer. Use the lasso tool to create outline, fill with color and change opacity to 50 percent. Repeat for second layer. Add "brads" by creating an additional layer using the elliptical marquee tool to draw the circle. Use the drop shadow and bevel and emboss for a realistic feel. Insert photos. Create title and add outer glow to text. To re-create this layout manually, attach layers of torn vellum with pink brads to an enlarged black-and-white photo. Place three cropped pictures on vellum with foam adhesive. To create title, print mirror image of title on white cardstock; cut with a craft knife and adhere to picture.

Amy Alivis, Indianapolis, Indiana

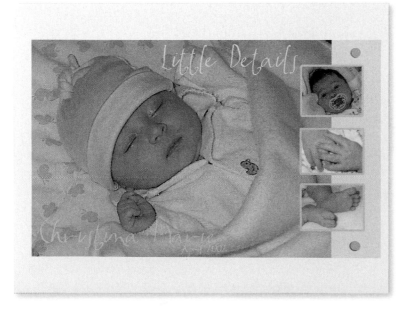

My Girl Madison

This layout displays many techniques reflecting quintessential vintage appeal. Tear corners from patterned paper (Anna Griffin); mount on pink paper. Machine stitch along straight and torn edges and place strand of craft pearls (source unknown) along torn border. Write journaling on pink paper and add clock face (7 Gypsies) accent tied with ribbon. Lightly rub coffee bean stamp pad around edges; gently roll back for aged appearance. Mount photo on patterned paper (Anna Griffin) using photo corners. Place on textured cardstock (Bazzill) rubbed with ink pad; sew around edge. Repeat techniques throughout layout. Embellish with ribbon flowers, die cut (Anna Griffin) and letter stickers (Anna Griffin). Create tag by layering various-size tags from a tag template (Deluxe Designs). Coat the metal plaque (Making Memories) with pigment powder (Ranger), followed by perfect medium (Ranger). Paint the footprints with pigment powder.

Vanessa Spady, Virginia Beach, Virginia

Sugar and Spice

Tammy created an eclectic layout of her eight-month-old daughter by incorporating collaged pieces representing all things feminine. Start with gingham paper (Pebbles Inc.) and layer various pieces of patterned paper (Keeping Memories Alive, Making Memories) and specialty papers (Bazzill, Magenta). Tear and chalk edges to create a frame within the page. Embellish with eyelet words, eyelet charms, page pebbles (Making Memories), ribbon flowers (Hirschberg Schutz & Co.), letter stickers (Provo Craft), brads, beads, buttons, charms and nailheads.

Tammy Jackson, Spring Hill, Florida
Photos: Lisa Prillaman

Always Keep a Secret Spot

Leah's page of embossed paper enhanced with white stamping ink provides just enough contrast and texture for visual interest. Gently rub white stamping ink on raised portions of black embossed paper (Club Scrap); place on metallic embossed paper (Club Scrap). Cut black paper (Club Scrap) into a photo frame; crumple, flatten and rub with stamping ink. Adorn top of frame with fibers and adhere in back. Print journaling onto silver metallic paper and attach with nailheads (Jest Charming).

Leah Yourstone, Issaquah, Washington

God Made
The World...

Martha incorporates splashes of color to contrast the soft hues of a black-and-white photo. Double mat enlarged photo on textured green cardstock (Bazzill) and blue cardstock; adhere to white background. Crop sections from watercolor patterned papers (Wordsworth, Creative Imaginations, Karen Foster Design); affix along left side of page and accent with fibers. Print journaling on white cardstock; double mat on blue and green textured cardstock and mount to page.

Martha Crowther, Salem, New Hampshire
Photo: Cristina Arroyo Falucho, La Mirada, California

Danielle, 7   *Haley, 7*

Blowing Bubbles

The enlarged picture on this summer layout draws attention to the subject, allowing the photo to become the central focus of this graphic page design. Enlarge focal photo to 8 x 10"; mat on white cardstock and adhere to left page. Create first part of title by cutting a title printed on white cardstock with a craft knife. Cut strips of light blue and white papers; adhere near title on left page and across bottom and middle of right page. Affix poem stones (Creative Imaginations) for the second half of title to maintain the look of bubbles; add paper circles with pen detailing to accent white paper journaling block. Add journaling along bottom of journaling block to complete.

Michele Woods, Worthington, Ohio

Wagon

Polly uses bright colors and bold patterns in her layout, appealing to the sense of summer fun her daughter Lauren has with her wagon. Fold pieces of green textured cardstock (Bazzill) over all four corners of red polka-dot patterned paper (All My Memories) and adhere to back of page, imitating the look of photo corners. Wrap plaid ribbon (Offray) around top and bottom of main picture. Double mat on green and red cardstocks, tearing along bottom edges. Place mounted photo on a lighter shade of textured green cardstock (Bazzill) layered on the patterned background paper. Create title using template (EK Success); decorate with green buttons and outline with black pen. Accent layout with page pebbles (Creative Imaginations) and letter stickers (Colorbök, Creative Imaginations). Complete page by adorning tags (Avery) with decorative punches (EK Success) and buttons.

Polly McMillan, Bullhead City, Arizona

Catalina

Using monochromatic and neutral color schemes allows the photos in Michaela's layout to become the visual focal point. Begin with a light green textured cardstock background (Bazzill); cover left half with dark green textured cardstock (Bazzill). Mat both photos on light green cardstock and place in opposite corners. Use letter stamps (PSX Design) and a black pen on specialty paper (Artistic Scrapper) for journaling and title blocks; mount to bottom right corner of page. Enclose additional journaling within a torn strip of light green textured cardstock; adhere to specialty paper. Fold each side and secure with ribbon (Offray) and hemp adorned with heart charms (Alphabet Soup).

Michaela Young-Mitchell, Morenci, Arizona

May Your Worries Be Like Dandelions

Melissa gave her page unique accents by duplicating an element of a meaningful picture and hand stitching her own dandelion design. Layer torn strips of red cardstock and red gingham paper (Frances Meyer) at the top and bottom of a navy background page. Mount focal photo and square-punched photo elements off-center. Sketch image of dandelion on paper; hand stitch with three strands of white embroidery floss. Journal on vellum with black pen; place atop stitched image. Attach with star brads (Magic Scraps).

Melissa Boyd, Douglasville, Georgia

Daughter

Heather's interactive page incorporates love notes to her daughter placed inside a charming paper bag border. Mat photo on blue cardstock and tear along bottom edge. Adhere matted photo to brown cardstock, leaving room at the bottom for embellishments and title. Decorate with heart shapes (Westrim) and handmade embellishments; attach with heart brad (Creative Imaginations). Create title on white paper using letter stamps (PSX Design) and red stamping ink; affix with brads (Creative Imaginations). Construct border using tiny paper bags. Place handwritten notes on tags embellished with metal washers and paper yarn (Making Memories). Further adorn paper bags by tearing white squares, chalking edges and layering with heart shapes (Westrim).

Heather Preckel, Swannanoa, North Carolina

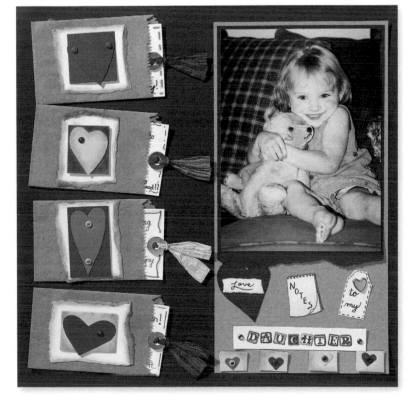

Wish

By artfully combining vintage and modern accents, Lara creates an eclectic look for her layout. Layer torn pieces of striped and paisley patterned papers (Robin's Nest) for background. Create a metal mesh border (Scrapyard 329) layered with letter stickers (EK Success), extreme eyelets (Creative Imaginations) and buttons along the left side of page. Use product packaging (7 Gypsies) to frame section of picture and to use as a tag in upper right corner. Ink edges of frame with brown ink and stamp with quote stamp (Uptown Design). For tag, ink edges with brown ink; layer with "Wish" sticker (Making Memories). Embellish bottom right corner with skeleton leaf (USArtQuest), watch face (7 Gypsies) and additional letter stickers.

Lara Gustafson, Glendale, Arizona

Where the Wild Things Are

Inspired by the patterned paper blocks used to mat her photos and dress up her title, Joan created complementary cardstock to enhance her design. Treat textured cardstock (Bazzill) by holding red ink pad and rose chalk ink pad perpendicular to paper and dragging toward the center. Print journaling on red textured cardstock (Bazzill); mount to treated paper. Adhere pictures to cardstock and patterned paper (Sarah Lugg). Create title by layering patterned paper on treated cardstock; print. Accent title and bottom left corner with a tag and hearts cut from patterned paper (Sarah Lugg).

Joan Fowler, Kingston, Ontario, Canada

Moon and Stars

Using a quote by Les Brown and two favorite pictures of her daughters, Tammy created a page comprised of star-inspired collage elements. Mount strips of torn and inked specialty papers (Solum World) on patterned paper (Scrap-Ease) to resemble a frame. Apply wired gold ribbon and decorative paper cord (Yasutomo) across the top and bottom to create a border. For title and word accents, randomly place expressions throughout page using letter stickers (Provo Craft), page pebbles (Making Memories), alphabet letters (Foofala) and eyelet letters (Making Memories). Adorn top right corner with star and moon (Wallies). Embellish page with gold wire heart (Card Connection), beads and charms.

Tammy Jackson, Spring Hill, Florida

Sisters

This simple and elegant layout showcases the special connection between two sisters. Tear patterned paper (Mustard Moon) and mount to terracotta background. Tear long strip and angular piece of vellum (Provo Craft) by hand; machine stitch angular shape to top of background paper and strip to bottom of page. Mount picture on specialty paper (source unknown) accented with eyelets in each corner; place in center of page. Accent with skeleton leaves and wire dragonfly (handmade). Create title and cut out with craft knife.

Evana Willis, Huntley, New Zealand

Little Girl Princess

In an effort to showcase her grand-daughter's personality in her elegant wedding attire, Linda combined several black-and-white and color pictures. Tear specialty paper (source unknown) diagonally, placing one piece in the bottom right corner of background paper; turn remaining piece so that corner will be in top left of adjoining page. Double mat photos on white and black cardstocks, arranging systematically on page. Print journaling onto vellum and title onto white cardstock; tear title words and mount to torn green cardstock. Embellish with large and small daisy punches (Carl) and tiny flower punch (All Night Media) centers. Randomly place heart brads (Hyglo/American Pin) throughout.

Linda Beeson, Ventura, California

Alexandra, 9

Poppy

Stacy cleverly used the design of her background patterned paper (Club Scrap) as a title, incorporating its text within the layout. Mount photos on dark green cardstock with main photo double mounted on torn vellum. Place stickers (Club Scrap) on punched dark green cardstock squares; embellish with decorative nailheads (Jest Charming); adhere around corners of both pages. Journal on torn vellum; mat on green cardstock. Complete with memorabilia pocket (3L) containing pressed flowers on right page.

Stacy Hackett, Murrieta, California

Her Laughter

Chris showcases her daughter's contagious laughter by incorporating lighthearted pictures with torn and crumpled design elements. Begin with a yellow cardstock background. Tear blue cardstock; crumple and smooth flat. Attach near the lower third of background page; place metal photo corners (Making Memories) at each side for accents. Tear a piece of patterned vellum (Paper Adventures) along one side and place toward top of layout; adorn with metal corners. Tear a second piece of patterned vellum on both sides; layer on blue cardstock. Triple mat photo on white, blue and green cardstocks; accent with metal snaps (Making Memories). Create the look of water droplets by cutting shapes from blue cardstock, outlining with a black pen and crumpling for added texture. Complete page with journaled rectangular block slid partially under patterned vellum. Affix cardstock "droplets" to the side.

Chris Douglas, East Rochester, Ohio

Mercedes, 5

Parris, 3

The Moments You Remember

Lisa's use of black and pink cardstocks creates a striking contrast, making the colors in her playful pictures pop. Tear strips of patterned paper (Colorbök) to use as embellishments for left page. Mount two photos on pink paper and adhere two unmatted photos directly to black background pages. Create bead (Blue Moon Beads) accents for torn patterned paper strips on left page, and vertical photo mat on right page by stringing beads on wire. Poke through papers and adhere to backs of pages. Journal on patterned paper and vellum. Embellish right page journaling block with pink fibers and secondary photo with floral photo corners (EK Success). Finish left page with additional pink fibers.

Lisa Francis, New Castle, Indiana

Sunny Smiles

Using a build-a-page kit (EK Success), Denise creates a well-designed page by incorporating her own unique artistic touches. Place patterned vellum on green striped patterned paper; mount on brown cardstock and use triangle shapes of patterned paper as photo corners. Tear plaid paper; roll back edges and layer with sunflower border strip. Place remaining accents on foam spacers for dimension; embellish tag with fibers. Print journaling onto vellum and adhere over premade embellishment to finish.

Denise Johnson for EK Success

Like the Air You Sustain Me

Focusing on a single enlarged photo is a simple but ultimately striking approach to page design. Heidi's well-composed layout begins with checkered patterned paper (Cherished Memories). Tear vellum "pockets" and hand stitch with green embroidery floss to green cardstock; mount on patterned paper. Adorn each pocket by placing a flower (Heidi's own design) inside. Double mat photo in varying shades of green and affix to dark green mat. Accent corners and bottom edge of dark green cardstock with flowers (Family Treasures) punched from rice paper. Print journaling onto vellum and hand stitch to photo to complete.

Heidi Schueller, Waukesha, Wisconsin

Babies Touch the World With Love

Karen's title was the only journaling needed to express the sweet innocence and love of this little newborn. Begin by double matting photo on cream and pink colored cardstocks; print name and date onto cream cardstock, leaving room at the bottom for embellishing. Adhere small silver beads to the paper and thread with pink and silver fibers. Attach three small buttons (Making Memories); mount on patterned paper background (Pebbles Inc.). Construct title strip by printing mirror image of "babies"; cut from pink cardstock using craft knife. Print remaining word on patterned paper (Pebbles Inc.) and pink cardstock. Attach with brads; place on tag (Making Memories) and embellish with metal charm (Making Memories). Thread wire through silver and letter beads to create "world." Embellish border by attaching torn strips of blue patterned paper (Pebbles Inc.) with silver eyelets (Making Memories). Finish by repeating fiber technique vertically along the border; mat on pink cardstock and adhere to page.

Karen Cobb, Victoria, British Columbia, Canada

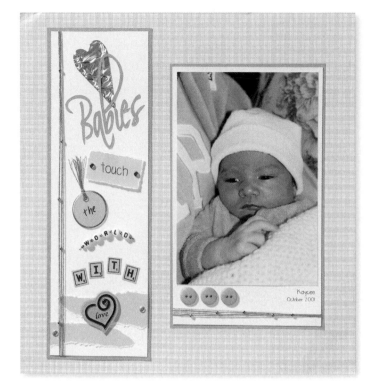

You Can Learn A Lot of Things...

It's not always a faux pas to mix several different patterns! Here Heather successfully combines various patterned papers to create a layout rich in both texture and detail. Basket weave four coordinating patterned papers (Printworks) for background; create purple border for bottom and right side of page with suede paper (K & Company). Embellish metal-rimmed tags (Making Memories) with punched photos and journaling. Hang from fibers and attach to back of page. Computer print journaling on vellum; use spray adhesive to mount.

Heather Uppencamp, Provo, Utah

Sweet Sisterhood

Heidi captured tender moments shared by her daughters and featured them in her layout about sisterhood. Layer daisy patterned paper (Frances Meyer) on blue cardstock background. Single and double mat photos on pink metallic paper and green cardstock. Create a ribbon border across the top of the page and hang metal-rimmed tags (Making Memories) from fibers. Embellish tags with flowers cut from patterned paper (Frances Meyer). Create journaling block by scanning image of intertwined hands; enlarge and lighten using photo-editing software. Print title and journaling on top of image; print on high-quality paper. Adhere to page and embellish with pink ribbon.

Heidi Bishop, Rockford, Illinois

Picture Perfect

With classic embellishments and personalized artistic touches, Polly uniquely displays several picture-perfect shots of her daughter. Use three coordinating tone-on-tone patterned papers (Lasting Impressions) to create background. Mount on white cardstock equal distances apart. Tear photos along edges; mount with green eyelets and brads. Embellish white tags (Lasting Impressions) with metal plaques (Making Memories), pictures, circle tags (Making Memories), heart fabric sticker (EK Success), dragonfly (Hirschberg Schutz & Co.) and ribbons (Offray); adhere to bottom of page. Create flower accent with green paper and blue button and mount above tags. Construct title block by cutting a rectangle with decorative scissors (Fiskars). Create tag with green paper; chalk edges and embellish with metal charm (source unknown), white tags (Avery) and gingham bow. Finish by adorning white tags with green brads (Making Memories), title and pen detail.

Polly McMillan, Bullhead City, Arizona

Karissa

Subtle color and soft lines contribute to Maureen's delicate and endearing baby page. For left page, tear gray patterned paper (Kopp Design) and adhere to pink textured cardstock (Bazzill). Mount photo on solid gray paper and adhere to background. Punch squares from gray paper and layer with punched patterned paper squares. Place date and age information in conchos (Jest Charming) and affix to center of squares. Print journaling block on vellum and adhere to left page with spray adhesive. For right page, create calendar (Broderbund); print milestones and events on vellum, placing polka-dot patterned paper (Lasting Impressions) behind for emphasis. Accent with additional gray and patterned paper square punches embellished with metal flowers (Making Memories) in bottom corner of page.

Maureen Spell, Carlsbad, New Mexico

Now I Lay Me Down to Sleep...

Martha created a soft feminine feel to her design by incorporating lace and beaded accents. Frame patterned paper (Hot Off The Press) with black cardstock. Create border along left side and bottom edge with lace. Double mat photo on black and yellow cardstocks. Accent with yellow butterfly (Martha Stewart). Adhere small picture behind slide mount and attach with foam spacer. Embellish slide mount with fibers. Print journaling on vellum. Tear and chalk edges of vellum and accent with fibers.

Martha Crowther, Salem, New Hampshire
Photos: Tracey Olson, Norman, Oklahoma

Wrapped in a Kitten-Soft Blanket

Using a single black-and-white photo of her niece bundled and softly sleeping, Amy captures all that is warm and snugly about a newborn baby. Begin by printing journaling on top half of speckled pink cardstock (Making Memories); mount photo. Tear out a portion of the bottom third of the pink cardstock. Punch hearts (EK Success) from removed section of pink cardstock. String embroidery floss through punched hearts; affix to top and bottom pieces of pink cardstock. Mount to full sheet of white cardstock.

Amy Alvis, Indianapolis, Indiana

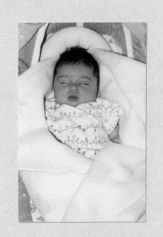

Wrapped in a kitten-soft blanket and snuggled in the bassinet, a sweet baby dozes contentedly. Soon, though, the first steps and the first words will come.

By Angela Thomas Guffey

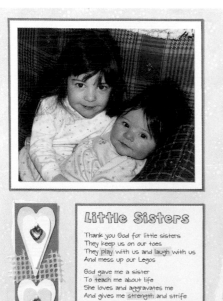

Little Sisters

Thank you God for little sisters
They keep us on our toes
They play with us and laugh with us
And mess up our Legos

God gave me a sister
To teach me about life
She loves and aggravates me
And gives me strength and strife

Thank you God for little sisters
They are special as can be
Don't mess with my little sister
Or you'll have to deal with me
~ Annabel Henley

Little Sisters

An endearing poem provides the perfect page addition to sweet pictures of these two sisters. Begin by layering torn mesh paper (ANW Crestwood) and torn patterned paper (source unknown) on green cardstock; add triangle shapes adorned with buttons (Making Memories) to top and bottom right page corners. Hand tear tag from white paper and chalk edges with green chalk; adorn with heart eyelets (Making Memories) and fibers. Create heart page accent by layering green cardstock, mesh paper, heart die cuts (Sizzix) and charms (source unknown). Embellish journaling block by highlighting significant words with pink colored pencils; mat on green cardstock.

Tracey Pagano, North Caldwell, New Jersey

Simply Noelle

Inspired by this picture of her daughter, Carol created a title page for her album using the definition of her name for journaling. Layer torn strips of coordinating patterned papers (Paper Fever) on striped paper background (Paper Fever). Mat photo on yellow paper and adhere to page. Create title using various metal letters (Making Memories); affix with eyelets. Accent page with yellow flowers cut from patterned paper, a single metal flower (Making Memories), buttons, a brad for flower centers and date eyelet (Making Memories). Journal definition block and adhere to page to complete.

Carol Darilek, Austin, Texas

Nurture

Heather created a vintage feel in her layout by using old embellishments and distressing paper. Begin with pumpkin-colored paper for page background (Kopp Design). Cut applicable definition from patterned paper (7 Gypsies) with a craft knife; mount on white cardstock. Adhere to strip of definition paper with foam spacers; mount to bottom of page. Tear section of plaid patterned paper (Kopp Design) along bottom edge and place measuring tape along the side. Mount to left half of background page. Mat photo on white paper and adhere to page off-center. Create title with letter stickers (Creative Imaginations) and frame with black strips of cardstock. For journaling block, crumple white cardstock; rub with orange chalk. Mount journaling and embellish with buttons (Jesse James).

Heather Preckel, Swannanoa, North Carolina

The Essence of Beauty

Dawn chose earth-toned colors that harmonize with black-and-white pictures of her niece on the beach. Treat textured cardstock (Bazzill) by wiping with white ink pad across pages. Age striped paper (Chatterbox) with sandpaper; mount, covering just over half of background for left page and layer atop script paper (7 Gypsies) block for right page. Sand patterned paper (SEI) for photo mats for all three photos; mount to pages. Create triple-matted triangle border from patterned papers for top of left page; dangle starfish and sea horse charms (Charming Spirits) on tulle strung through eyelets. Embellish right page photo mat with glass bottle (7 Gypsies) filled with clear micro beads and tiny photo strung from tulle. Print journaling on transparency; treat with silver metallic rub-ons and adhere to page with extreme eyelets (source unknown).

Dawn Hinck, Englewood, Florida

Rachel, 9

Spice!

Sugary-sweetness isn't all that is nice about girls. Sometimes showing what they are really made of requires a girl to exhibit a little attitude! Though they may be small in stature, girls walk tall when they are strong-willed, self-assured, and irresistibly sassy. It's this spicier side of a girl's personality that brings out the wild angel, dare devil, diva or drama queen responsible for so many of her crazy, zany moments. Maybe she's the type to sashay with a silly hand-on-hip saunter, or like a true Hollywood siren, to peer mysteriously from beneath glamorous sunglasses. Maybe she likes to sport spunky ensembles of her own choosing that represent her personality and individual style. Or maybe she simply exudes vivaciousness in her boundless energy and fierce love of life. Most often, there is just something in the eyes that signifies a wild spirit and untamed heart. "Spice" is the characteristic that confirms girls are unapologetically "all-that" and then some, and only adds to their irresistible charm.

Hailee, 4

The knowingness of little girls is hidden underneath their curls.
—*Phyllis McGinley*

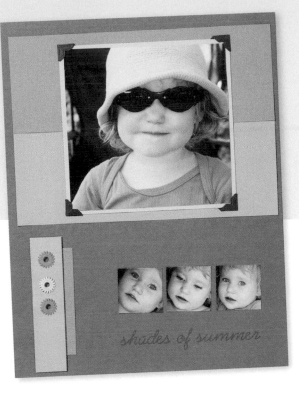

Shades of Summer

Cheryl used striking colors to complement those found
in her pictures, making for a graphic and well-composed
page. Print title on textured dark pink cardstock (Bazzill).
Mat photo on lime-colored textured cardstock (Bazzill) and
adorn with black photo corners; mount to two melon-
colored textured cardstock (Bazzill) blocks and adhere
to page. Square-punch three photos and mount to page
above title. Complete page with lime and melon textured
cardstock strips embellished with flower eyelets (Impress
Rubber Stamps).

Cheryl Overton, Kelowna, British Columbia, Canada

Sweet Side, Silly Side

Jodi created a whimsical page featuring two distinct sides of her daughter's personality by incorporating a flip-
style cardstock panel and word stickers. Mat floral patterned paper (Colorbök) to speckled pink cardstock.
Place various "sweet" and "silly" sticker words (EK Success, It Takes Two, Me & My Big Ideas, Scrapbook Mania,
Wordsworth) to the appropriate half of the page. Double mat photos using pink and orange and white and orange
cardstocks; adhere. For flip-style panel, mount patterned papers (KI Memories, K & Company) on both sides
of a 6 x 12" piece of pink cardstock; cut windows with a craft knife to highlight individual words when panel is
flipped. Print journaling on vellum; tear edges and accent with chalk; adhere to applicable side of panel. Hinge
panel to background page by making three small slices at the center of the background page at the top, middle
and bottom; thread ribbon (Offray) to hinge the flip page and accent with buttons (Making Memories).

Jodi Amidei, Memory Makers Books

Silly

Little embellishing is needed to complement this contagious smile. Keep the focus on a great photo with simple cardstock strips and a straight-forward title. Print journaling onto terracotta cardstock; tear an oval from the bottom and mount orange cardstock behind. Cut uneven strips of yellow cardstock and mount horizontally across top third of page. Mat photo on orange cardstock and layer on top of strips. Use a craft knife to cut title from yellow cardstock; adhere across torn oval.

Michele Woods, Worthington, Ohio

Pick Some Daisies

Lisa chose patterned papers to add to the whimsical theme of the poem she chose for her journaling. Tear green daisy patterned paper (Provo Craft) and layer to create border along top and bottom edge of yellow daisy patterned paper (Provo Craft). Print journaling on polka dot patterned paper (Lasting Impressions); mount on orange cardstock and adhere to background page. Triple mat photo on yellow cardstock, green patterned paper (Provo Craft) and orange cardstock. Mount over part of journaling block and adhere to page. Create title tags on polka-dot patterned paper matted on green cardstock. Finish with gingham ribbon (Offray). Accent with tag embellished with name and date on torn yellow cardstock mounted to orange cardstock and tied off with ribbon.

Lisa Simon, Granville, Ohio

Mommy...

Sheila's recording of her daughter's daily aspirations in journaling makes for a fun page both will enjoy reflecting upon in the future. Mat patterned vellum (Autumn Leaves) on brown cardstock. Apply a large rivet (source unknown) to a strip of brown cardstock; string with fibers and adhere to right side as a border using foam spacers. Print title and journaling on light brown paper; rub edges with metallic rub-ons (Craf-T). Mat photos on light and dark brown cardstocks and mount to journaling block using self-adhesive foam spacers. Add name to bottom of journaling block using letter stamps (Hero Arts) and accent with tiles (Magic Scraps).

Sheila Boehmert, Island Lake, Illinois

A New Perspective

In this simple layout with a lot of emotion, Kimberly expresses the unique relationship between her husband and their daughter in detailed journaling. Print title vertically along textured green cardstock (Bazzill). Affix photo to top of background page. Print journaling on tan cardstock and layer atop green cardstock. Accent with torn patterned paper (Scrap-Ease) on opposite corners of page; chalk edges using green chalk.

Kimberly Lund, Wichita, Kansas

In Stitches

Maria creates visual interest and dimension by weaving vibrant fibers around brads throughout her design. Punch squares (Punch Palace) out of various colors of textured cardstock (Bazzill). Place colored brads in the center of each square; randomly mount to white paper. Weave pink, yellow, green and orange fibers around brads in crisscross pattern. Tear pink and green cardstock for photo mats and mount pictures; adhere to layout using foam spacers.

Maria Newport, Smyrna, Georgia

Maasai Turns 3!

The "terrible twos" may be the infamous time of self-expression and rebellion for most children, but Maria has discovered her daughter Maasai's third year to be her most assertive period yet. Mat pink dot paper (Kangaroo and Joey) on raspberry dot paper (Paper Patch). Mat photos on yellow cardstock and mount askew across left side of page. Construct yellow tag using a template (Deluxe Designs). Print journaling on vellum; place over tag and attach with pink eyelet. Embellish with fibers and pen detail. Mat raspberry patterned paper squares atop yellow cardstock squares; string fibers through pink eyelets. Further embellish with candle cut-outs (EK Success).

Maria Newport, Smyrna, Georgia

Katie

Reflecting her niece's femininity and flare for fashion, Sahily created a bold design with unique papers and soft textures. Layer a strip of stripe-patterned paper (Colorbök) and a strip from a gift bag on pink patterned paper (Cross My Heart). Accent with butterfly element cut from gift bag; mount on yellow textured cardstock (Bazzill). Mat focal photo on textured brown cardstock (Bazzill) and wrap fiber around bottom; adhere to page. Offset remaining photos on textured blue cardstock (Bazzill) and mount in opposite corners. Journal on yellow cardstock and affix to page with brads.

Sahily Gonzalez, Miami, Florida

Simply Corinne

Deborah used colors that coordinate with the various pictures used, making for a colorful and playfully candid page design. Use various shapes of pink, purple and blue cardstocks as color blocks on black paper. Accent blocks with metal flowers (Making Memories), stickers (EK Success), eyelets, jewels (Suze Weinberg) and mesh (drywall tape). Add title on vellum and attach to page with eyelets. Stamp journaling with letter stamps (Hero Arts).

Deborah Hamlin-Karalun, Highland, California

Extraordinary

Simple lines and clean design are a perfect combination in Becky's vellum-block layout. Print journaling on blue vellum using various font styles; affix to cream cardstock with silver brads. Mount photo on green vellum; overlap blue vellum and adhere with brads. Layer tan vellum over blue vellum; affix with brads. Embellish with circle tags (Avery) with circle punched (Marvy Uchida) cardstock and patterned paper (Club Scrap) centers.

Becky Thompson, Fruitland, Idaho

Daisy Daze

Debra adds instant creative flare to the focal photo of her layout by offsetting the photo mats. Manufacture your own daisy stamp using a die-cut machine, daisy die and craft foam. Stamp green cardstock background with watermark ink (Tsuki-neko) for a subtle watercolor effect. Crop three photos and double mat on white and dark green cardstock panel and use as a border. Triple mat focal photo on white, yellow, and dark green cardstocks; offset the yellow piece. Accent with flowers made from aforementioned stamp and shrink plastic (Lucky Squirrel) that has been shrunk and colored with green and yellow chalk. Create title using strips of vellum and ABC stamps (Stampcraft); mount above and below focal photo.

Debra Lyle, Elida, Ohio

In the Spring...

Amy re-creates the aftermath of a day spent playing in the dirt by using brown chalk to imitate its effects. Print journaling on speckled cream cardstock; mat on brown cardstock. Cut square pieces of craft foam to create a personalized "dirt" block shadow stamp. Use watermark ink (Tsukineko) and color with chalk. Place letter stickers (Creative Imaginations) within blocks to spell "dirt." Stamp handprint (Inkadinkado) on white cardstock using watermark ink (Tsukineko); color with brown chalk. Cut into angular shape and mat on brown and tan cardstocks. Triple mat photo, alternating shades of brown; place off-center within the page.

Amy Stultz, Mooresville, Indiana

Bright

Becky used bold colors and graphic design elements to complement the playful personality of her daughter. Create background by layering yellow and maroon cardstock strips on a black cardstock background. Punch circles from yellow, maroon and teal cardstocks; layer on black cardstock strip. Mount one photo on teal cardstock; leave two photos unmatted and adhere all to page. Cut thin strips of maroon, teal and yellow cardstocks and adhere along top and bottom of page. To complete, highlight edges of definition sticker (Making Memories) with teal ink pad for journaling block.

Becky Thompson, Fruitland, Idaho

I Want To Be a Superstar!

Jane subtly hand-tinted her daughter's sunglasses in the color of her papers for an added stylistic element. Begin with a light purple cardstock background. Cut a lavender strip of cardstock for right side of page; create a watercolor effect by using watermark ink (Tsukineko) and randomly stamping stars (Inkadinkado). Print journaling after ink has dried; mount to background page. Mat photo on lavender cardstock, then on white handmade paper (source unknown); tear bottom edge. Place white eyelets in top corners and string with fiber. "Hang" picture from white brad. Accent layout with star brads and additional fibers.

Jane Rife, Hendersonville, Tennessee

Silly Girl

Renae took inspiration from her goddaughter's outfit to choose complementary shades of blue and yellow for her page. Layer yellow cardstock on light blue cardstock background; mount one photo to strip and another to bottom right corner. Hand stitch X's with blue paper yarn (Making Memories). Create tag and layer with blocks of light blue and dark blue cardstocks and title printed on vellum. Accent with journaled cardstock strip, handmade dragonfly, heart button (Jesse James) and paper yarn. Create journaling block by mounting journaled cardstock strips on a dark blue cardstock block; embellish with buttons (Jesse James).

Renae Clark, Mazomanie, Wisconsin

Ashley Anne

Sherri used monochromatic colors and elegant accents to place emphasis on the photos and journaling. Mat light blue paper on textured dark blue cardstock (Bazzill). Double mat photos on various shades of blue cardstock. For focal photo, tear paper along bottom edge and mount torn piece slightly lower. Using a needle and fiber, stitch pieces together and accent with skeleton leaves (www.skeleton-leaves.com); adhere all photos. Use a craft knife to cut title; mount on dark blue border and attach with brads. Embellish brads on one end with fibers (Wal-Mart). Create journaling block on right page by mounting skeleton leaves to light blue cardstock panel matted on dark blue cardstock. Print journaling on vellum; layer on skeleton leaves and attach with brads. Accent with fibers and charm (A Charming Place). To finish, adorn each page with squares punched from light and dark blue cardstocks; embellish with skeleton leaves and journaling.

Sherri Brady, Victoria, British Columbia, Canada
Photos: Sue Street, Parksville, British Columbia, Canada

Alexandra, 9

The Pits

Diana cleverly incorporated patterned paper and page accents to complement her daughter's ribbon-tied pigtails and bowl full of cherries. Layer cherry paper (Creative Imaginations) with grid die-cut paper (Die Cuts With a View). Triple mat focal photo on coordinating cherry paper and black and red cardstocks. Mat secondary photos on red and white cardstocks; adhere all photos. Layer cherry paper and square punched photos on square tags (Making Memories); attach scalloped eyelet (Stamp Doctor), polka-dot ribbon (Offray) and adhere. Accent with cherry stickers (EK Success). Complete page by creating title with rubber stamp (source unknown).

Diana Graham, Barrington, Illinois

The View

Maureen created a playful feeling in her layout by using bold colors and sharp, asymmetrical angles. Begin with red cardstock background. Cut strips of primary-colored cardstocks to frame page's interior; accent each strip with fibers and adhere. Crop photo at skewed angles and triple mat on black paper and patterned papers (Doodlebug Design) and green cardstock following the same skewed angles. To create title, layer with letter stickers (Creative Imaginations) and journaling printed on vellum (Paper Adventures) strip. Print journaling on yellow cardstock; crop at skewed angle and mount on black cardstock with mini brads. Accent layout with wire house embellishment (Westrim).

Maureen Spell, Carlsbad, New Mexico

Sticky and Sweet

Debbie showcased several pictures of her daughter enjoying the experience of eating cotton candy by creating a progressive border along the bottom of her spread. Distress background paper (Karen Foster Design) by aging with sandpaper and steel wool. Layer patterned paper (Karen Foster Design) on yellow paper; tear, roll edges slightly, chalk and adhere along bottom half of each page. Mount photos atop patterned paper. Double mat one photo on patterned paper and yellow paper; distress and chalk using aforementioned technique. Affix photo at an angle to left page. For title and journaling blocks, print on yellow paper; distress and chalk. Crumple journaling block; flatten and adhere to right page. Accent both blocks with flower die cuts (Sizzix), repeating distressing technique.

Debbie Kuehl, Green Bay, Wisconsin

Faces of My Child

Maria combined bold colors and several textures to create a striking layout to showcase her daughter's animated expressions. On red cardstock, melt black extra thick embossing powder along bottom and right side of page. Layer two corners with paper yarn (Making Memories) and accent with swirl paper clips (Making Memories). Tear photos, mat on torn white paper and embellish with eyelets. Mount to background in a collage and create name along one photo using letter stickers (Me & My Big Ideas). Create title using black cardstock and lettering templates (Scrap Pagerz) for "faces"; accent with extra thick embossing powder and silver eyelets. Use letter stamps (Hero Arts, Pixie Press) for second part of title. Print journaling on white paper; tear edges and accent with extra thick embossing powder; affix to page. Complete page by accenting with white buttons.

Maria Newport, Smyrna, Georgia

Sarah, 11

Itsy Bitsy Teenie Weenie...

To complement the design of her daughter's zany zebra-striped swimsuit, Pam utilized torn strips of patterned paper and vibrant embellishments throughout her layout. Layer black cardstock background with torn strips of pink textured cardstock (Bazzill), zebra-striped paper (NRN Designs) and star-patterned paper (Daisy D's). Slightly roll edges of pink cardstock. Print title on stickers (NRN Designs), matting last word on zebra embellishment and green cardstock; adhere to top of left page. Accent with additional black-and-white embellishments (KI Memories) and stickers (NRN Designs). Mat all photos on green cardstock and adhere. For right page, print journaling on vellum; frame with green cardstock. Crop several photos and affix to background page.

Pam Easley, Bentonia, Mississippi

Warning...I Have an Attitude

Using a unique approach to scrapbook design, Sam created her layout using 8½ x 11" paper turned horizontally and embellished with products from outside the scrapbook store. Vertically mat a trimmed piece of 8½ x 11" blue cardstock to yellow cardstock. Punch squares along bottom edge of greeting card (Target); adhere strip of blue cardstock underneath card cover and stamp "attitude" using letter stamps (PSX Design). Adhere greeting card across blue cardstock. Wrap top of photo with fibers; create embellishments by removing the posts from square and circle thumbtacks (Target) with wire cutters. Adhere to greeting card. Frame a cut section from card with a black slide mount adorned with dog tag (All The Extras) and mini brad (All The Extras). Finish title with letter stickers (source unknown), stamping (PSX Design) and handwriting. Accent page with fibers and additional thumbtack embellishments.

Sam Cousins, Trumbull, Connecticut

Our Material Girl

Drawing from the eclectic look of her daughter's Madonna-esque dress-up outfit, Peggy created a layout with whimsical style and flare. Mount dark pink squares on plaid patterned paper (Doodlebug Design). Double mat photo on pink and silver papers; adhere to center of background. Journaling with black pen using a template as a guide (Chatterbox). Using the same template, trace pattern with a pencil and stitch with white embroidery floss. Create title by printing mirror image onto silver paper; cut with a craft knife. Print name on vellum and adhere in corner.

Peggy Kangas, Pepperell, Massachusetts

Sugar and Spice

Jane hand-tinted her daughter's baseball cap, lending a feminine flare to well-composed black-and-white photos. Begin with dark gray cardstock background. Print journaling on pink cardstock; stamp dragonfly (Stampcraft) above journaling. Layer atop cardstock background and place fibers along the length of each side. Double mat photos on light gray cardstock and pink silk paper (Frances Meyer). To create title, print mirror image on pink cardstock and cut with a craft knife.

Jane Rife, Hendersonville, Tennessee

Today You Are You

Pink hues, a young girl peering from beneath sunglasses, and a playful quote make for a catching combination. Triple mat focal photo on white and pink cardstocks and mount askew to dot patterned paper (Making Memories). Tear secondary photo; mat on torn pink cardstock. Frame layout with fibers strung through scalloped eyelets (Stamp Doctor) at each corner of page. Print journaling on vellum; mount to background with white eyelets. Create date accent on pink paper and mount to circle tag. Finish tag with fibers.

Jane Hasty, Chicago, Illinois

I Feel Pretty

Tiffany created a whimsical yet feminine design by combining striking patterns and brightly colored fibers. Layer dot paper (Treehouse Designs) on swirl paper (Stampin' Up!) to create background pages. For left page, mount a strip of pink cardstock to swirl paper; accent with fibers. Print journaling on white cardstock; mat on yellow cardstock and affix to page. Accent with metal-rimmed tag embellished with date; adhere with foam adhesive. Mount photos askew to background. For right page, triple mat photo on yellow, pink and white cardstocks. Embellish with circle tag adorned with ribbon flower (Offray); hang from a clear button. Mount photo and string fiber below, securing behind back of page. Print journaling on pink paper. Mount secondary photo to page to complete.

Tiffany Roberts, Bonney Lake, Washington

Danielle, 7 and Dakota

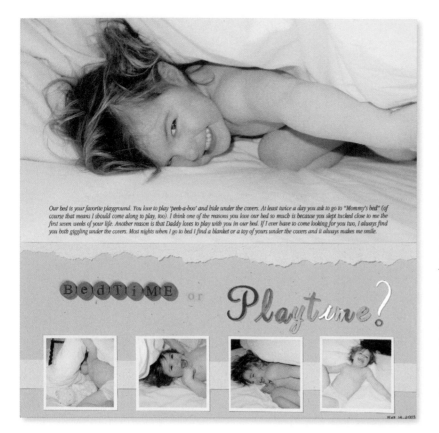

Our bed is your favorite playground. You love to play 'peek-a-boo' and hide under the covers. At least twice a day you ask to go to "Mommy's bed" (of course that means I should come along to play, too). I think one of the reasons you love our bed so much is because you slept tucked close to me the first seven weeks of your life. Another reason is that Daddy loves to play with you in our bed. If I ever have to come looking for you two, I always find you both giggling under the covers. Most nights when I go to bed I find a blanket or a toy of yours under the covers and it always makes me smile.

Bedtime or Playtime?

Digitally altering photo sizes using photo-editing software programs adds instant dramatic impact to a page. Begin with a periwinkle cardstock background. Tear yellow paper along edge and mount across top two thirds of page. Scan photos and use a computer software editing program (Adobe Photoshop) to enlarge and crop photos as desired. Print journaling onto enlarged photo; print all photos onto photo paper and cut. Mount large photo on yellow paper and attach square photos to yellow paper strip along bottom of page. Create title with metal letters (Making Memories), letter stickers (SEI) and eyelet letters (Making Memories).

Christine MacIlvaine, Oakland, New Jersey

Funny

Ari chose square letter stickers and a square-cropped photo to complement the graphic design of her patterned paper. Print journaling on brown cardstock. Tear patterned paper (Ivy Cottage Creations) along top and bottom; adhere to page background. Mount focal photo on patterned paper and secondary cropped photo in lower right corner. Create title using letter stickers (Creative Imaginations) inside squares of patterned paper.

Ari Macias, Staten Island, New York

My Zoe...
You are the biggest goofball ever! We were sitting on the deck, doing our usual nothing. I asked you, Zo, can I take your picture? You said SURE and then gave me this classic pose. I almost had an asthma attack I laughed so hard. The best part was that after that "look" you gave me the biggest smile. I love this picture because it shows your littlegirlness...your chipped pretties, your cute pigtails! I love ya!

Divas

Vintage textures and embellishments combine to make a layout dedicated to two modern divas. Adhere torn patterned paper (K & Company) strip to edge of left page and in a panel for right page; mount on dark brown cardstock. For photo mats, stamp script image (Timeless Images) on pink paper with coffee bean ink; mount photos and adhere to background pages. Construct collage tag on left page by layering newsprint paper (7 Gypsies), postcard ephemera (Leeco), rickrack sticker (SEI), poem stones (Creative Imaginations), heart paper clip (Making Memories) and knob (Leeco) on vintage tag (Foofala). Affix to torn patterned paper. Print journaling block and title onto transparencies. Stamp script image on natural netting (source unknown) and place behind title. Ink edges of pink cardstock and smear with atelier molding compound (source unknown). Embellish with flowers cut from patterned paper (K & Company); place transparency on top and attach with rickrack sticker (source unknown). Further accent layout with small patterned paper circles, brads and string.

Melissa Martin, Sydney, Australia

Lilo Skirt

Valerie combines whimsical colors, patterns and embellishments with playful pictures of her daughter. Adhere strips of patterned papers (KI Memories, SEI) to top and bottom of blue cardstock background. Mat photos on white paper and yellow patterned paper (KI Memories). Embellish photos with grass skirt straw to form photo corners and hula skirt. Accent hula skirt with flower buttons (Jesse James) and affix to bottom of single photo. Adhere all photos to page. Create journaling block by printing on patterned paper; adhere beneath photos. For title, handcut "Lilo" from red paper and create "skirt" using letter stickers (Doodlebug Design) and letter embellishments (Beary Patch). Use silhouette flower punch (Family Treasures) to create lei title accent. Place vellum word sticker (Bo-Bunny Press) on tag (Making Memories) and attach with jute and flower brad (Provo Craft). Embellish layout with additional tags (Making Memories) with solid- and patterned-paper centers and flower accent (Colorbök) with button center.

Valerie Salmon, Carmel, Indiana

Kite

Drawing from the colors in her daughter's clothes, Diana creates a well-balanced design in complementary hues. Mat yellow cardstock on blue paper. Cut four strips of patterned paper (source unknown) and frame outside borders; embellish corners with daisy punch (Family Treasures) and blue eyelets. Triple mat larger photo with patterned paper, yellow cardstock and blue cardstock; cut with deckle-edge scissors. Mat second photo on blue cardstock; create handmade photo corners from yellow cardstock; detail with blue pen. Cut the title with deckle-edge scissors and embellish with tiny daisy punches (Family Treasures), yellow eyelets and white pen detail. Layer title with journaled vellum block. Construct kite using patterned paper, flower punches, strips of yellow and blue cardstock and eyelets. Finish kite with knotted string and mount with foam spacers. Complete page with journaling printed on vellum and torn into a strip; affix beneath larger photo.

Diana Graham, Barrington, Illinois

The Expression

Lisa chose monochromatic colors and graphic design concepts to enhance a single special photo and journaling. Vertically print title in gray ink on side of light green cardstock. Adhere picture to left side. Print journaling in gray ink on a darker shade of green cardstock. Tear out top portion of journaled paper to create frame for picture; roll edges slightly. Mount on background paper with mini eyelets (Making Memories); dog-ear one corner. Thread wire through eyelet to attach charm.

Lisa Stanley, San Lorenzo, California

Why I Wish You'd Never Grow Up

Clean lines and a bold design allows journaling and pictures to be the primary visual draw in Kimberly's layout. Print name and age on top corner of light brown cardstock. Cut dark brown cardstock in half and mount on light brown cardstock, covering half of each page. Print journaling on patterned paper (Mustard Moon). Cut into tag shape using template (Scrap Pagerz); embellish with fibers. Mat photos with pink and yellow cardstocks; place on layout and overlap with journaling tags.

Kimberly Lund, Wichita, Kansas

Baby Face

With minimal embellishments and soft complementary hues, Vikki assures nothing will compete with her black-and-white photo—and those pinchable cheeks! Adhere strip of pink paper horizontally across silver paper. Mat photo askew on black paper. Set silver eyelets on bottom corners. Use letter stickers (Creative Imaginations) for title inside vellum metal-rimmed tag (Making Memories); dangle on beaded chain through eyelets. Journal on pink paper. Dangle heart charm (Making Memories) from beaded chain through silver eyelet. Mat askew to black paper and affix to page.

Vikki Hall, Rogers, Arkansas

It Is a Happy Talent...

Bonnie successfully collages textures and patterns without compromising the central focus of these bath-time pictures. Tear strip of rubber duck patterned vellum (Autumn Leaves) and adhere to top of background patterned paper (Mustard Moon). Using a craft knife, silhouette cut photo and strip of patterned vellum; mount to torn strip of black paper and adhere to background. Mat photos on torn black paper and mesh blocks (Magic Mesh); accent with string and jewelry tags (American Tag Co.) stamped with date. Create title block by machine stitching yellow paper to patterned paper (Mustard Moon) and adding sticker quote (Creative Imaginations). Layer on mesh and accent with snaps. Print journaling on vellum. Accent layout with clear picture pebbles (Making Memories) and circle tag (Making Memories) embellished with sticker (Creative Imaginations).

Bonnie Perry, Chico, California

Princess Audrey

Inspired by the jeweled crown atop her daughter's head, Holle creates a regal feel by accenting her layout with rhinestones, beads and wire. Mat photo and journaling printed on pink paper on dark pink cardstock; adhere to background patterned paper (KI Memories). Double mat wire "Princess" title (Creative Imaginations) on light pink and dark pink cardstocks. Use lettering template and craft knife to create name (Wordsworth) from pink cardstocks. Accent with tiny flower punches (EK Success). Print accent journaling on vellum (Close To My Heart); adhere behind slide mounts (Jest Charming). Embellish with rhinestones and wire hearts (Westrim).

Holly VanDyne, Mansfield, Ohio

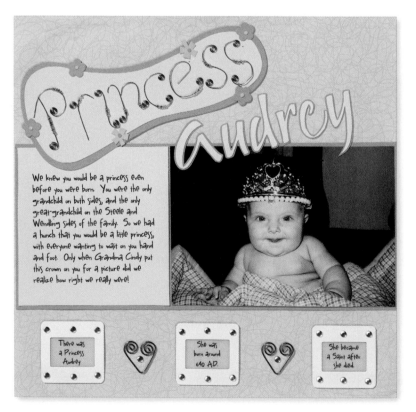

Mood Swing

The textures and colors of these outdoor photos makes mesh paper and sanding and chalking techniques the perfect approach for Tracey's layout. Mount pictures on green cardstock. Layer top and bottom with mesh paper (Magenta); accent with dragonfly (Stampcraft) mounted on sanded paper. Construct tag by layering cream cardstock, metal letters (Making Memories), letter stickers (Robin's Nest) and finishing with fibers. Mount tag with foam adhesive. Tear and chalk edge of cream cardstock to create border. Print journaling on vellum; attach with nailheads (Jest Charming) and fiber. Mat remaining photo on green cardstock.

Tracey Pagano, North Caldwell, New Jersey

Yummy in Yellow

Denise used rich yellows and abundant textures to create her tactile composition. Mount light yellow embossed paper (Provo Craft) onto black cardstock. Punch three holes on each side and randomly lace ribbon (Offray). Mount stitched paper (Creative Imaginations) on black cardstock; adhere to embossed paper with foam adhesive. Create title by printing on transparency (Artistic Expressions) and embossing with extra thick embossing powder to set ink. Affix to paper with black brads. Create laced embellishment by mounting embossed paper to black cardstock. Punch oval holes (McGill) in equal distances along inside edge of mat. Mount papers on foam adhesive. Start at the bottom and weave as if lacing a shoe.

Denise Tucker, Versailles, Indiana

Kellie, 11

Carlie

Dana printed her pictures in sepia tone, lending an earthy feel to her design to be carried over into her choice of paper hues. Use a color-blocking template (Deluxe Designs) and patterned papers (Magenta, O'Scrap) to dress up green cardstock background pages and cream cardstock. Accent with flower punch art (Marvy Uchida) and eyelets. Embellish further by stitching various blocks with embroidery floss, stringing on charms (All The Extras) and beads. Print journaling on vellum; attach with brads. Print the reverse image of a font for the title and cut with a craft knife.

Dana Swords, Fredericksburg, Virginia

All Girl?
Not Quite!

Using feminine floral prints in combination with brown cardstock cleverly showcases this little girl's preference for getting dirty over acting dainty. Tear patterned paper (Anna Grifffin) and mount on textured cardstock (Bazzill). Mat photo on patterned paper (Anna Griffin); accent with metal corners (Making Memories). Dog-ear one corner and affix with flower eyelet (Making Memories). Layer bow (Anna Griffin) on pink patterned paper; adorn title double-matted on cream-colored paper and patterned paper (Anna Griffin). Print journaling on vellum and cream cardstock. Mount on squares of pink patterned paper and accent with flower eyelets.

Maureen Spell, Carlsbad, New Mexico

Sitting Pretty

The striking look of black-and-white photos provides a pleasing contrast to the patterned papers of this garden-themed page. Mat white cardstock on green cardstock. Punch square shapes (Marvy Uchida) out of floral patterned paper (EK Success) and mat with green cardstock squares. Adhere photos across bottom of page. Layer top and bottom of page with torn patterned vellum (EK Success) attached with snaps. Print journaling on white cardstock; mat with green cardstock. Accent small picture with metal frame (Making Memories). Complete page with journaled embellishment (EK Success); tear bottom edge and mat with green cardstock.

Pam Easley, Bentonia, Mississippi

We're in Love With You Too

Bright colors and jewel embellishments complement Maria's pictures of her daughter happily dining in her tiara. Tear pieces of light pink cardstock and layer on dark pink cardstock. Cut a strip of purple paper and adhere across the tops of both pages; accent with rhinestones. Mount cropped photos to both pages. Print journaling on pink paper. Use a template (Deluxe Designs) to create tags using pink and purple paper; layer and attach with eyelets. Finish with small purple squares embellished with rhinestones.

Maria Newport, Smyrna, Georgia

Hailee, 4

Madison Is Love

Vanessa chose striking patterns and Valentine-inspired page accents to help express her adoration for her daughter. Mount pictures on coordinating pink paper (KI Memories) and adhere to patterned paper (KI Memories). Accent both pages with embellishments (KI Memories); adorn tag with decorative cord (source unknown). Use letter stickers (Creative Imaginations) to create the title.

Vanessa Spady, Virginia Beach, Virginia

Girls Just Wanna Have Fun

With their many talents and diverse interests, girls have fun engaging in numerous hobbies and activities. Whether involving computer keyboards or surfboards, ballet slippers or soccer cleats, rumbling four-wheelers or razor scooters, girls answer the call of adventure and the opportunity to display their skills with zest and determination. So much more than just pretty faces, girls are spirited competitors, motivated team players and intellectual problem-solvers. Some girls revel in the healthy rivalry and action provided by sports like soccer and softball. Some would rather exuberantly rally their favorite players from the sidelines. Many girls prefer the creative outlets that art, music and crafts provide. And still others are simply always in search of good old-fashioned fun through exploration and ever-changing adventures. Regardless of what activity they choose to engage in, the fun-loving nature of girls guarantees good times. As their unofficial anthem playfully declares, "girls just wanna have fun!"

Haley, 7

Little girls, like butterflies, need no excuse.

—*Robert Heinlein*

Skate On

Kelly utilized paper scraps and customized her design with direct-to-paper stamping techniques. Layer various pieces of torn paper and mulberry scraps on background paper until covered; mat with black cardstock. Wipe and blend with several colors of stamping ink. Tear and chalk edges of several photos, mounting some on torn and chalked paper strips. Randomly layer additional photos and torn paper strips throughout page. Use letter stickers (Sticker Studio) for title and accent with smiley face nail heads (JewelCraft). Wipe and blend inks again, applying some directly to photos. Print journaling on green vellum; tear and chalk edges and adhere to page with smiley face nail heads.

Kelly Angard, Highlands Ranch, Colorado

The Girl's Got Kick!

Kelly added a feminine punch to an athletic page by creating dimensional paper flower embellishments. Mat orange patterned paper (Provo Craft) on black cardstock. Tear several strips of white cardstock; add color to edges with orange chalk and black ink. Layer on page to create background. Adhere black gingham ribbon (Offray) both vertically and horizontally across page, intersecting along bottom left side. Mount focal photo on white cardstock that has been inked and chalked. Adhere remaining photos at angles to page, tucking edges into torn strip background. For flower embellishments, tear various-sized circles from orange patterned paper (Provo Craft); chalk and ink edges. Layer circles to create paper flowers. Roll edges and adorn with various black buttons. Print journaling onto transparency; attach under ribbon. Create title with letter stickers (Creative Imaginations, Me & My Big Ideas, Mrs. Grossman's) to complete page.

Kelly Angard, Highlands Ranch, Colorado
Photos: Megan Galgano, Highlands Ranch, Colorado

OLE!

Maria added soft, subtle touches using chalking techniques and patterned vellum for journaling. Chalk edges of speckled cream cardstock (Provo Craft) and layer on red cardstock. Print journaling on patterned vellum (source unknown); accent with ribbon flower (Card Connection) and adhere with spray adhesive. Double mat focal photo on black and red cardstocks; layer partially over vellum. Mount remaining photos on red cardstock strip and detail with chalk.

Maria Williams, Cary, North Carolina

The Joy of Dance

Lisa chose colors that complement her pictures and feminine embellishments that flatter her design. Layer peach cardstock with embossed vellum (K & Company). Create title and journaling; print on green vellum and attach to cardstock using eyelets. Mount focal photo on pink cardstock and create photo corners using green velveteen paper (Wintech) and corner punch (Marvy Uchida). Cut secondary photos into tag shapes adorned with fibers; tuck slightly inside vellum journaling panel. Accent with fibers and punched leaves (Family Treasures, Punch Bunch).

Lisa Simon, Granville, Ohio

Danielle, 7   Haley, 7

Beginnings

Mary-Catherine creates a truly unique accent using mulberry paper to construct stage "curtains." Begin with plum-colored cardstock background pages. Create title by printing the mirror image of font onto white cardstock; cut with craft knife and adhere vertically along side of left page. Accent title with buttons (Hillcreek Designs). Mount focal photo on pink and sage cardstock blocks matted with white cardstock. Write date along bottom corner of photo. For right page, create photo mat by printing journaling on sage cardstock; adhere photo. On patterned vellum (Fiskars), print journaling and layer over ballerina silhouette clip art (Broderbund). Tear pieces of mulberry paper (Leapenhi Paper Design) to create top of the stage curtain. Construct sides by fan-folding pieces of mulberry paper and tying with fiber and beads. Embellish vellum tags (Making Memories) with stickers (Paper House Productions). Layer on mulberry paper, tie with fibers, and attach with buttons (Hillcreek Designs). Accent star punch (Emagination Crafts) by off-setting from square punch (Punch Bunch) and adorning with buttons.

Mary-Catherine Kropinski, Maple Ridge, British Columbia, Canada
Photos: Sylvain Senez, Pitt Meadows, British Columbia, Canada

Let Your Life Lightly Dance...

Combining bold colors and collaged page accents adds visual interest and texture to Michaela's design. Tear green textured cardstock (Bazzill) and layer on berry textured cardstock (Bazzill). Cut edges of picture with decorative scissors (Fiskars); mount on page. Print title quote on clear transparency; mount with pink mini brads (ScrapArts). Embellish green cardstock strip using square metal-rimmed tag (Making Memories), white tag (Avery), mesh (Magenta), ribbon flowers (Offray), buttons (source unknown), circle clips, charm and fibers. For shaker box accent, dry emboss leaf on green cardstock that has been cut into a tag shape; embellish with fibers. Create box with foam tape and acetate; enclose beads (Wal-Mart). Accent shaker box with patterned paper (Karen Foster Design), buttons, ribbon flower (Offray) and mesh (Magenta).

Michaela Young-Mitchell, Morenci, Arizona

Tutu I Remember...

Tina utilized Christmas decorations to create the perfect accents for her page. Tear and chalk edges of patterned paper (K & Company); mount on pink cardstock. Double mat photo on white and pink cardstocks. Tear top edge of pink cardstock and embellish with glitter and star eyelet (Making Memories). Adhere to page. Journal in black pen around torn edge of paper and beneath photo mat. Stamp title with letter stamps (PSX Design). Embellish layout with wire fairy, snowflakes and metal tags (Making Memories) decorated with stickers (Paper Adventures) strung across page on silver cording.

Tina Coombes, Langley, Berkshire, England

Sophia

Jodi chose bold and beautiful colors to showcase the special qualities present in a little girl named Sophia. Frame blue cardstock with rust-colored cardstock to create background pages. For left page, triple mat photo on cream, plum and rust cardstocks; adorn bottom of photo mat with silver swirl clips. Journal on blue cardstock with silver pen; double mat on plum and rust cardstocks. Use a craft knife to create an open frame comprised of plum and rust cardstocks. Wrap wire around frame and affix with foam adhesive. Within frame, attach metal letters (Making Memories) with silver brads. For right page, double and triple mat photos using cream, plum and rust cardstocks. Repeat frame technique using square punches (Marvy Uchida) for accent on second page. Journal inside frames using silver pen.

Jodi Amidei, Memory Makers Books

Kellie, 11

Friendship

Jessie used an oversized picture that becomes the focal point of her design, combined with unique accents and concealed journaling. Mount enlarged picture on right side of teal cardstock background. Affix small paper bag containing tag (Westrim) in left corner. Lay gingham ribbon along edge of enlarged photo and over paper bag. Layer with remaining two photos. Accent with definition stickers (Making Memories) embellished with flower eyelet (Making Memories) and cameo spiral clip (7 Gypsies). Frame metal letters (Making Memories) affixed to ribbon with metal belt loop (7 Gypsies). Print journaling on white tag and conceal in paper bag; finish with gingham ribbon.

Jessie Baldwin, Las Vegas, Nevada

Nature Walk

Carol created a unique accent by tucking her journaling inside an embellished paper bag. Layer focal photo on cream mulberry paper and brown cardstock; adhere to skeleton leaf patterned paper (EK Success). Double mat secondary photo on brown cardstocks and adhere. Create journaling accent printed on brown paper adorned with letter tiles (source unknown). Place journaling in paper bag (Paper Adventures) adorned with premade title embellishment (EK Success), rivets (source unknown) and twine. Rubber stamp date (Office Max) on bag. To complete, affix a few actual skeleton leaves (Graphic Products) along top border of patterned paper to blend naturally with paper design.

Carol Darilek, Austin, Texas

Ropin'
Some Hearts

Jane stays true to the Old West appeal of this layout by using vintage papers and aged accents. Layer brown textured cardstock (Bazzill) on patterned paper (7 Gypsies) to create background for both pages. For right page, crop top photo and adhere; mount larger photo to patterned paper. Set eyelets in corners of remaining photo and adhere to brown cardstock. Create page accent by layering brown corrugated paper (DMD) with patterned paper strip, jute strung through eyelets, cropped photos and metal letters (Making Memories). For left page, mat single photo on patterned paper and mount square-cropped photos on brown cardstock. Embellish envelope with eyelets, jute and metal star accent (Making Memories) and square punched photo. Use letter stamps (PSX Design) to create title.

Jane Hasty, Chicago, Illinois

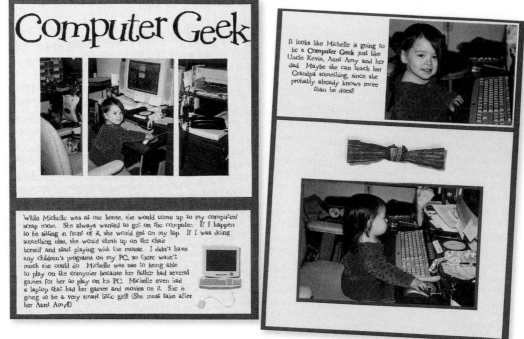

Computer Geek

Amy used color-blocking techniques, bold colors and clean lines to design this layout inspired by a pint-size computer wiz. For left page, cut photo into thirds; mount on light pink textured cardstock (Bazzill) and adhere to berry-colored textured cardstock (Bazzill). Create title with letter stickers (Creative Imaginations). Print journaling on light pink textured cardstock. Adhere to berry cardstock and accent with computer embellishment (EK Success). For right page, print journaling onto light pink cardstock; affix photo and mount to page. Mat second photo on berry cardstock and again on light pink cardstock; adhere to background. Accent with bow made from paper yarn (Making Memories) to complete.

Amy Alvis, Indianapolis, Indiana

Sarah

Amy used contrasting colors and simple techniques to create a visually appealing, photo-focused layout. Tear one side of red paper strip; mount as a border along top portion of black background page. String beaded chain through metal dog tags (Chronicle Books). Adhere by pushing wire through front of layout and twisting in back. Mount two photos on red cardstock, tearing along one side. Crop third photo and adhere to page unmatted. Create title by printing the mirror image of a font on cardstock; cut with a craft knife.

Amy Brown, Payette, Idaho

www.little-fingers.com

Cheryl used an oversized picture to capture her daughter's small hands stretching to maneuver a computer mouse. Create background by layering a black cardstock panel on maroon cardstock. Adhere a thin cream-colored cardstock strip at the seam. Mount pictures on cream cardstock and affix to background. To create title, place letter stickers (Provo Craft) on large focal photo. Create journaling block by printing on three different colors of cardstock. Cut two journaling blocks and piece on top of third. Accent with star brads (Making Memories) mounted to small cardstock squares.

Cheryl Uribe, Grapevine, Texas

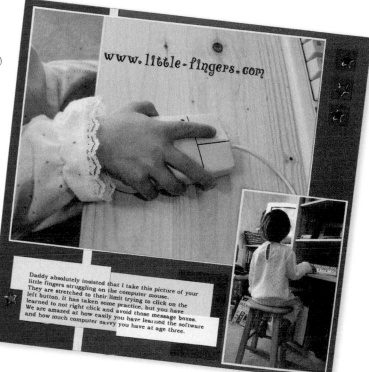

The Art In Me

Becky included her daughter's self-portrait by scanning the image and adjusting the size to work with her layout. Create script patterned paper by using a stamp (A Stamp in the Hand) on mushroom-colored paper; tear on both sides. Tear a section from brown cardstock; layer with script paper on black cardstock background. Journal on tan paper; tear and chalk edges. Attach journaling block with copper brads (Impress Rubber Stamps). Print a muted version of photo on matte finish photo paper; adhere on right side of background. Scan and resize original artwork using computer software program; mat on brown cardstock and affix to page. Design tag using script stamp, passport stamp (Impression Obsession) and letter stamps (PSX Design). Layer with label (Dymo), mesh, and letter tags (Hot Off The Press) attached with copper brads. Finish with gingham ribbon (Offray).

Becky Thompson, Fruitland, Idaho

Together

Katherine combines several subtle textures to create dimension in her layout. Frame textured light green cardstock (Bazzill) with a slightly darker shade of textured green cardstock (Bazzill) to create background pages. For left page, print journaling on cream-colored textured cardstock (Bazzill), leaving room for matted photo. Detail edges with black pen and affix to background with mini eyelets (Making Memories). Ink corrugated cardboard (DMD) and apply extra thick embossing powder; heat to set. Mat photo on dark green textured cardstock (Bazzill) and adhere to corrugated cardboard mat. Mount to journaling block. Mat three cropped photos on dark green cardstock and use as a border along bottom of page. Embellish with cardstock strips. Create title using polymer clay (Polyform Products) stamped with letter stamps (PSX Design) and flower (Jim Stephan) using stamping inks. Bake as directed, cool and rub with metallic rub-ons; attach with brads. For right page, mount photos on dark green cardstock; embellish one photo with mini eyelets and adhere all to page. Square punch two photos and mount on light green cardstocks. Adhere cardstock strips along right side of page. Create tag by journaling on cream cardstock and cutting tag shape; embellish with clay accent created using aforementioned technique. Finish with an eyelet and gingham ribbon.

Katherine Brooks, Gilbert, Arizona

Kellie, 11

Bobby Sox Minis

Diana embellished the buttons used on her page to resemble softballs for a truly unique accent. Begin with two black cardstock background pages. Cut top border from yellow cardstock and mount to top of left background page. Create title using letter templates (Scrap Pagerz) and black and yellow cardstocks. Embellish vellum tag (Making Memories) using embroidery floss to stitch baseball threads along top and bottom. Add letter stickers (EK Success) and attach with a black brad. Affix photo above baseball patterned paper block (Creative Imaginations). Layer with journaling printed on vellum affixed with buttons (Making Memories). Mount square-cropped photos and journaling on black cardstock and accent with buttons and tags (ACCO) attached with embroidery floss. Adhere black photo mat to yellow cardstock layered with an additional picture. Repeat same techniques for right page.

Diana Hudson, Bakersfield, California

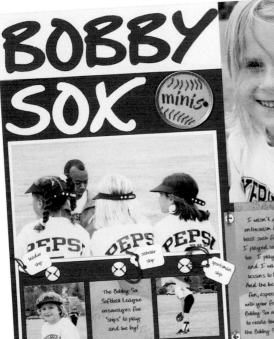

Soccer

Brandi captures her daughter in action on the field with her photos and keeps them the central focus with her clean composition. Tear two pieces of vellum and layer on blue patterned paper (Pebbles Inc.) background pages. Use red patterned paper (Pebbles Inc.) to mount and accent all photos; embellish with silver brads (Making Memories). Create journaling captions using letter stamps (Hero Arts) and black ink on cream-colored cardstock; tear ends. Create title with letter stickers (Making Memories). Showcase subject in one photo by cutting vellum center out of square tag (Making Memories); attach fibers to each side and adhere to photo mat with brads. Print journaling and tear each side before adhering to right page.

Brandi Ginn, Lafayette, Colorado

Hailee, 4

Haley

Lisa uses texture and shine to visually enhance the design of her sport-inspired layout. On textured black paper (Emagination Crafts), layer metal mesh strip (AMACO). Mount photo on glossy red paper (source unknown) and attach at an angle to layout. Decorate mesh with star wine glass charm (source unknown) and vellum tag (Making Memories) dangling from an eyelet adorned with rhinestone stars. Create title accent by using metal stamps on red craft metal (source unknown). Remove vellum center from metal-rimmed tag (Making Memories) and layer rim over metal title. Attach with silver brad and accent with baseball charms. Frame remaining square-cropped photo with square metal tag (Making Memories).

Lisa Francis, New Castle, Indiana

Soccer Star

Kim showcases a childhood picture of herself playing soccer along with meaningful journaling about her feelings toward the sport. Tear patterned paper (KI Memories) and layer on textured cardstock (Bazzill). Mount photos on black cardstock and adhere to page. Create title by altering letter stickers (Doodlebug Design, Wordsworth) and tag wear (Creative Imaginations) on vellum tags and background paper. Accent title with metal star (Making Memories). Print journaling on vellum and attach to layout.

Kim Haynes, Harrah, Oklahoma

When I was young, I was really into sports. I played basketball, soccer and softball. My all favorite though, was soccer. I had SO much fun playing for the 9 years that I did. I stared out playing Co-Ed, then moved on to a traveling all girls team. Although I wasn't as fast as most, I was actually very good! I spent most of my school years from third grade and on playing, then decided to quit my sophomore year in high school. I really regret quitting, to this day, I haven't told many why exactly I did. Truth is, I was quite a bit heavier than the other girls in H.S. and was very intimidated by the coach. I wish I had the confidence I do now back then; I could have gone pretty far with it. Pictures taken 8th grade (top) 5th (bottom)

Fishing

Dana utilized metal fish accents and fibers in various shades of blue to complement these shoreside shots of her stepdaughter fishing. Begin with a blue cardstock background. To create border, layer pieces of teal, torn purple, and blue cardstocks along left side of page. Adhere four blocks of mesh (Magic Mesh) at askewed angles throughout page. Create photo mats by blocking blue and purple cardstocks on teal mats. Embellish by stringing fibers, floss, beads (Crafts Etc.) and star button (Streamline) between two eyelets. Detail border by stringing fibers and floss through eyelets; decorate with handwritten tags (Making Memories, Sizzix) that have been chalked and detailed with black pen, star brads (Making Memories), circle paper clips and fish accents (Streamline).

Dana Swords, Fredericksburg, Virginia

Hooked on Fishing

Tammy incorporates fun fish tags taken from gift bags to provide for perfect page additions. Layer a thick strip of yellow cardstock on aquamarine paper. Print title and journaling on blue vellum; adhere to background with spray adhesive. Punch squares from teal paper to accent focal photo. Mount cropped photo unmatted to yellow cardstock strip. Frame small picture with slide mount (Club Scrap). Accent page with fish tags (source unknown) embellished with handcrafted hook (Artistic Wire) and java weave (Jest Charming). Create shaker box by placing shaved ice (Magic Scraps), micro beads (Embelleez), sequins and fish appliqué (Buttons Galore) in a resealable bag. Place bag behind teal tag and finish with fibers.

Tammy Jackson, Spring Hill, Florida

Surfer Girl

Heidi chose watermark and speckled patterned papers to carry over the shoreside feel of her pictures into her layout. For left page, tear edges of focal photo and layer on torn vellum and purple patterned paper (Making Memories). Mount matted photo on blue patterned paper (Making Memories). Create title with lettering templates (Scrap Pagerz); layer on torn paper and accent with purple eyelets. Crop photos and mount on purple patterned paper along bottom of page, over wavy sticker border (Me & My Big Ideas). For right page, print journaling on vellum; attach with eyelets. Crop photos, mat on purple patterned paper and adhere over wave border.

Heidi Dillon, Salt Lake City, Utah

Girls Can Do Anything Boys Can Do!

Margert chose a fun way to alter her grass-and-daisies patterned paper by "driving" an inked toy car across it, creating haphazard tire tracks. Enhance patterned paper (Karen Foster Design) by running a rubber-wheeled car over a stamping ink pad; "drive" it in several directions across page. Mat photo on white cardstock and adhere to page. Print title and journaling on vellum. Mat journaling block on white cardstock and accent with eyelets and fibers. Embellish layout with handcut daisies and plastic wheels (Matchbox).

Margert Ann Kruljac, Newnan, Georgia

And Away She Goes!

Cynthia cleverly incorporates several pictures in eye-pleasing sequential page borders. First, create tire tracks by randomly running a small rubber wheel from a toy car through watered-down black paint (Delta) and across blue cardstock background. Print title on green cardstock and journaling on blue cardstock. Randomly punch square shapes (EK Success) along strips of green cardstock. Mount pictures to blue cardstock background behind openings. Adhere both green border strips with foam adhesive for dimension. Mat larger photos and journaling block on green cardstock and adhere to page.

Cynthia Coulon, Provo, Utah

Scooter Princess

Inspired by her daughter's color coordination and love for all things purple, Maria chose several complementary hues to design her page. Create negative space at top and bottom of purple paper by tearing out sections; offset when adhered to white cardstock. Trim and frame on green paper. Use square punches to create frame accents. Link squares together by creating small slits; adhere along torn sections. For title, use letter stickers (Colorbök) placed inside squares. Double mat photo on white and green papers; adhere to page. Print journaling on vellum; layer over purple and green paint chips (Behr) and attach with eyelets (Making Memories).

Maria Williams, Cary, North Carolina

Bikin' Barbie Style

Jill used the vibrant, cheerful colors of her daughter's cherished Barbie bicycle to craft her layout. Frame patterned paper (Doodlebug Design) with white cardstock and attach with flower eyelets (Making Memories). Mat focal photo on white cardstock and leave secondary photo unmatted; adhere both to page. Print title and journaling on white cardstock. Create "Barbie" by printing the mirror image of font; cut out with a craft knife. Accent journaling block with dragonfly punch (Marvy Uchida) and butterfly sticker (EK Success). Create collage accent by layering mesh (Magic Mesh, Avant Card) on purple cardstock with date stamp. Add flower punch art (All Night Media, Family Treasures) adorned with glitter glue (Ranger). Create tag using template (Deluxe Designs), emboss with silver powder, layer with button (Making Memories), punches (EK Success) and finish with fibers. Embellish square tag (Making Memories) with buttons (Making Memories) and punch art.

Jill Fickling-Conyers, Fresno, California

Sarah, 11

Tri County Rebels

Pam used pompom-patterned paper and bold accents to help document her daughter's cheerleading days. Frame patterned paper (Scrappin' Sports & More) on blue and red cardstocks for background pages. Print journaling blocks on patterned paper; mat on blue and red cardstocks and adhere to pages. Double mat single photo on white and red cardstocks and adhere to left page. Mount three unmatted photos and one square-cropped photo mounted on white cardstock to right page. Print title blocks on transparencies; mount with clear photo corners. Embellish layout with vellum circles decorated with buttons (Making Memories).

Pam Easley, Bentonia, Mississippi

She's a Lady

Despite mud created by rainy days, softball practice continued as usual and Sharon showcased the messy results on her layout. Layer torn strips of blue and terracotta cardstocks along bottom of each tan background page to create border. Embellish with fibers. Mat all but one of the photos on co-ordinating cardstocks; tear bottom edges. Print handwritten journaling on left background paper with blue pen. Create title by printing mirror image on blue cardstock; cut out with a craft knife and adhere to left page. Accent both pages with buttons.

Sharon Suske, Yates Center, Kansas

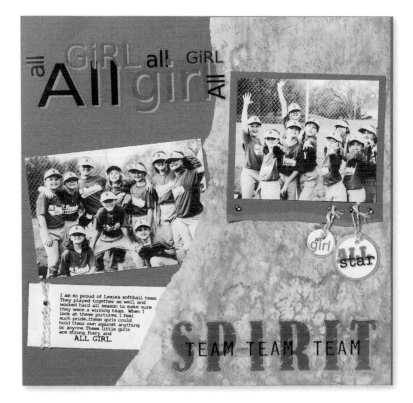

All Girl Team Spirit

Mindy used sassy colors to complement the spirited softball players celebrated in her layout. Layer torn patterned paper (Cut-It-Up) on textured purple cardstock (Bazzill). Apply title sticker (Creative Imaginations) over both papers. Mount one photo to purple background at a slight angle, tucking one corner under patterned paper. Mat second photo on purple cardstock and tear along bottom edge. Embellish with brads and accent metal-rimmed tags (American Tag Co.) with stickers (Creative Imaginations) and fibers. Print journaling on white paper; decorate with brads and fibers.

Mendy Douglass, Frankfort, Kentucky

Dedication

Cynthia personalized her journaling by including the definition of the quality she found most inspiring in her daughter. Begin with light green cardstock for background pages. For left page, print title on yellow patterned paper (Magenta). Layer with mesh paper (Magenta) and accent with page pebbles (Making Memories). Print journaling on green cardstock; adhere to background. Affix section of patterned paper (Magenta) to background; mount enlarged photo and accent with metal photo corners (Making Memories). Repeat layering techniques horizontally for right page. Mount two photos on patterned paper and cropped photos to yellow and green papers. Create tag embellishment from yellow patterned paper and light green cardstock; finish with eyelet, fibers and photo housed inside metal frame (Making Memories).

Cynthia Coulon, Provo, Utah

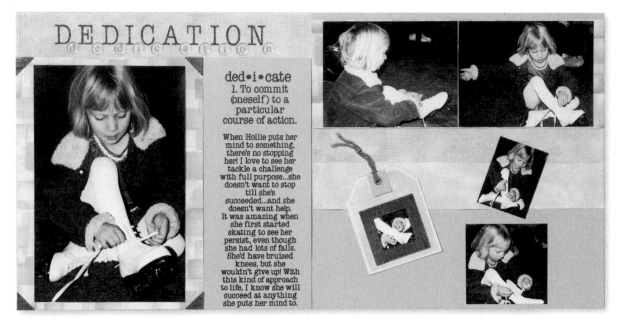

Friends...Scrappers

Lynn captured a moment between young friends during her daughter's seventh-birthday scrapbooking party. Tear flower patterned paper (Carolee's Creations) along top and bottom edges and mount to patterned background paper (Carolee's Creations). Mat photo on green-sponged patterned paper (Carolee's Creations) and adhere to page. Create title by printing mirror image on sponged patterned paper and cutting with a craft knife; embellish with mini brads (Carolee's Creations). Create a wavy strip from green sponged paper and string fibers and ribbon through metal flower accents (Carolee's Creations); embellish with flower adornment (Carolee's Creations) and brad and affix under title. Journal on white cardstock and mat with sponged patterned paper; accent with beads and wire word (Lynn's own design) mounted on striped accent (Carolee's Creations). Adhere green ribbon (Making Memories) border on bottom of page. Accent circle tags with metal flower (Making Memories), flower eyelet (Making Memories) and jewelry tag (Avery).

Lynn Whelan, Savannah, Georgia

Beautiful Music

Kelly's layout harmoniously blends charm and elegance with beautiful papers and artful embellishments. Tear edge of sheet music patterned paper (Design Originals) and frame on navy cardstock. Tear and ink edge of patterned vellum (Anna Griffin). Cut three sides to create window for picture and roll back vellum; secure with navy ribbon (Offray). Print journaling on brown paper; cut into strip and adhere to patterned vellum along with square-punched photo. Create title block by lacing pieces of torn embossed cardstock (source unknown) and music note patterned paper (source unknown) accented with eyelets and laced with ribbon. Use letter stickers (Creative Imaginations, Creative Memories) for title. Cut flowers from patterned paper (Anna Griffin) and place in music note patterned paper wrapped with ribbon.

Kelly Angard, Highlands Ranch, Colorado
Photos: Susan Sidebottom, Centennial, Colorado

Imagine, Create, Dream

Kelly created the quintessential artist's page by capturing a masterpiece in the making and by including an actual paintbrush as an embellishment. Frame patterned paper (Wordsworth) with purple cardstock. Mount two cropped photos on white paper; ink edges in various colors. Silhouette cut last photo and adhere along bottom of page. Create title by cutting words from patterned paper (Wordsworth); apply glue (Magic Scraps) and micro beads. Use letter stickers (Wordsworth) to spell remaining words. Create layered accent with silhouette cut handprint and paintbrush. Adorn with metal-rimmed tags (Making Memories) embellished with sticker (Wordsworth), butterfly accent (source unknown) and patterned paper (Wordsworth).

Kelly Angard, Highlands Ranch, Colorado

It's a Girl Thing

No matter the generation, there remain certain universally appealing and timelessly special experiences unique to girlhood. Even grown-up girls can recall engaging in the same imaginative games and social activities as young girls do today. Girls become rock stars when their hairbrushes transform magically into microphones and button-eyed stuffed animals morph into screaming star-struck fans. Doily-adorned tabletops host tea parties and transform dolls into refined ladies who lunch over imaginary chamomile and cookies. Cast-aside clothes from another time become glamorous gowns fit for beautiful fairy princesses. Far from encouraging slumber, sleeping bags provide perfect venues for staying up late and exchanging giggles and girl talk with treasured friends. These tried-and-true good times along with others involving make-up, hairstyles, shopping mall excursions and socializing are nothing less than girlhood rites of passage. Such decidedly female outlets of fun require no further explanation than simply stating…"it's a girl thing."

Alexandra, 9

Like star dust glistening on fairies' wings, little girls' dreams are of magical things.

—*Sherry Larson*

Fairy Princess

Lori created an ultra-feminine layout rich in texture by combining several techniques. Frame burgundy cardstock with pink vellum trimmed with decorative paper trimmer (Fiskars). Weave pink ribbon (Offray) through eyelets along border. Mat photos on white paper. Use decorative corner punch (Family Treasures) in each corner of mat; trim with decorative trimmer. Score white paper at corners and fold sides into the center. Mat on rose crackle patterned paper (Keeping Memories Alive) and adhere to page. Write journaling block with silver pen and mount on pink vellum. Accent with dragonfly (Sizzix) die cuts from vellum and patterned paper. Create title with metal letters (Making Memories) attached with pink eyelets.

Lori Haas, Battle Ground, Washington

Make Believe

Kate used clean lines and simple detail to bring the visual focus to the pictures of her daughter playing make-believe. Print journaling on pink paper. Mount pictures on plum cardstock; adhere in opposite corners. Create border in center of page by mounting patterned vellum (EK Success) on green cardstock. Soften vellum using acrylic paint (Plaid) and dry-brush technique. Accent design with flower stickers (EK Success).

Kate Nelson, Fountain, Colorado

Dress Up

Denise includes lace cut from an old dress to create an elegant overlay for this dress-up page. Begin by mounting two pictures on pink background paper. Lay sheer fabric over page, wrap around sides and adhere in back. Mount on black cardstock. Adhere remaining photos directly to fabric using foam adhesive. Create title tags (Making Memories) by printing letters on transparencies; sprinkle with thick embossing powder and heat to set. Cut into circles and attach to vellum tags with white eyelets; adorn with ribbon (Stampendous) and attach to layout with pink brads. Encase date using a bookplate (Ludwig Industries) attached with brads; adhere to bottom of left page. Print journaling on white cardstock; embellish edges with metallic rub-ons (Craf-T). Accent journaling block with charms (Boutique Trims) and metallic thread (Sulyn Industries). Mat journaling on black cardstock. Hand stitch fabric to page around journaling block with metallic thread to create pocket; slip journaling inside. Accent with ribbon flowers (Impress Rubber Stamps) and additional embossed tag.

Denise Tucker, Versailles, Indiana

Parris, 3

Mercedes, 5

Clothes Don't Make the Girl

This little girl's dress-up ensemble proves any outfit isn't complete without a little accessorizing—sometimes a fishing hat is just what a dress needs! Triple mat three photos on red or green paper, patterned paper (C-Thru Ruler) and white cardstock or vellum. Mat remaining photos on red paper. Adhere all matted photos to purple background paper. Print journaling on patterned vellum (C-Thru Ruler) and layer on patterned paper block; attach with flower eyelets (Doodlebug Design). Print title on patterned vellum; tear edges and attach to green cardstock with flower eyelets. Accent with flower stickers (C-Thru Ruler). Create pocket accent on right page by sewing patterned vellum to white cardstock mounted on patterned paper. Enclose a flower taken from dress-up outfit.

Gwendolyn Taylor, Sandy, Utah

All Dolled Up

Shelley chose fibers and created handmade accents to mirror all the details of her daughter's accessorized look—even shaping the beaded purse handle into an "M" for Mary, the glamour girl's name. Tear edge of patterned paper (source unknown); layer on pink vellum and pink cardstock background. Adhere fibers along torn edge. Triple mat picture on green cardstock, pink paper and mulberry paper (Pulsar), leaving room on right side for embellishing with white paper (Wintech) strip, star brads (Creative Impressions) and fiber. Print title on vellum; layer on torn pink paper and patterned paper. Embellish with heart eyelets (Eyelets, Etc.) and white paper. Layer letter stickers (Provo Craft) on mulberry paper, pink paper, white paper and pink mulberry paper; adhere to page. Create border by beginning with flowered ribbon. Create handmade dress using pink paper and flowered ribbon. Make purse embellishment with paper, decoupage adhesive and micro beads; shape handle from wire and string with beads. Triple mat both dress and purse with white paper, pink paper and patterned paper and mount to ribbon border. Complete with patterned paper strips matted on pink paper adorned with curled wire and eyelets.

Shelley Rankin, Fredericton, New Brunswick, Canada
Photo: Portrait Studio, Fredericton Superstore, Fredericton, New Brunswick, Canada

We Wait...

To accent her daughter's garden stroll in her dress-up clothes, Mary Anne created a collaged tag in bold, rich colors. Begin with wine-colored cardstock for page backgrounds. Print quote on patterned paper (Provo Craft); adhere to left page. Embellish with flower and heart eyelets (Making Memories). Create collaged tag using metal star (Making Memories), mesh paper (Magenta), tag (Avery), butterfly charm, feather and gems. Finish tag with fibers (Memory Crafts). Mount patterned paper strip to bottom of right page. Mat three photos on purple cardstock and leave two unmatted; adhere all to pages. Create journaling tags by printing on patterned paper; cut into tag shapes and accent with metal eyelets, gems and fibers.

Mary Anne Walters, Ramsdell, Hampshire, England

Friends

Cynthia creates fun and functional photo mats that artfully house photos and provide attractive page additions. Begin with butterfly patterned paper background (PSX Design). Create envelopes for photos using a template (Accu-Cut). Decorate envelopes with green and yellow mesh paper (Magenta) and butterflies cut from additional patterned paper (PSX Design). To create title, place letter stickers (Provo Craft) on punched square shapes (EK Success). Highlight squares by inking edges (Clearsnap). Print journaling on tan paper. Tear out and ink all sides of paper; adhere to page.

Cynthia Coulon, Provo, Utah

Touch, Smell, Pick, Give

Mary Anne captures her daughter stopping to smell the flowers amidst imaginative play outdoors and complements the photos with a whimsical quote. Layer green speckled patterned paper (source unknown) on dark green textured cardstock (Bazzill). Cut a wavy section from yellow cardstock to create a border for top of page and accent for journaling block. Mount two photos on wave border. Create double mat for focal photo using two shades of yellow cardstock; repeat wave accent across middle of mat, mount photo and adhere. Print journaling on light yellow cardstock; embellish journaling block with yellow border and cropped photo. Adhere to bottom corner.

Mary Anne Walters, Ramsdell, Hampshire, England

Mirror, Mirror, on the Wall...

Stitch work and intricate beading detail add extra feminine flare to Jane's page. Tear all four sides of purple vellum and hand stitch to purple cardstock using embroidery floss. Print journaling on white cardstock with purple ink. Mat photos to light purple cardstock and layer on three of the journaling blocks; adhere to page. Accent with pastel-colored beads (Crafts Etc.) strung on wire. Repeat beading technique and bend to shape to create page corner accents and flower embellishment.

Jane Rife, Hendersonville, Tennessee

She's All Dolled Up!

Inspired by words used in her title, Beth created a dimensional paper doll accent using her daughter's picture. Frame white cardstock with purple patterned paper (PSX Design) background. Layer with light purple paper and stamp (PSX Design) hat, crown, shoe and purse images using watermark ink (Tsukineko). Create border on white cardstock using swirl stamp (PSX Design) and black ink; color with markers and accent with flower stickers (PSX Design). Print journaling on light green paper; accent with stickers (PSX Design). Use paper doll template (PSX Design) to construct body; attach at joints with purple brads and silhouette-cut picture. Embellish accents with glitter glue. Mount three cropped photos on green and black paper; connect with purple wire. "Hang" pictures from flower sticker (PSX Design) mounted with foam adhesive.

Beth Clark for PSX Design, Santa Rosa, California

The Perfect Present

Mary-Catherine created a regal design using accents and colors to complement the fit-for-a-princess theme of her page. Begin with a purple textured cardstock background (Bazzill). Tear pink patterned paper (Karen Foster Design) and layer section vertically along side of left page and in horizontal strips across right page. Tear section of patterned vellum (Fiskars); cut window for picture using a craft knife. Frame window with gold embossing powder. Mount photo beneath and attach vellum with eyelets. Mount photo on pink cardstock and adhere to page. Print journaling on pink cardstock; mount on white cardstock. Create accent by coating slide mount (Kodak) with gold embossing powder and layering with metal number (Making Memories), jewels and shoe button (source unknown). Create title using letter stamps (Stampcraft) and metal jewel shapes arranged in "P" shape. Complete right page by mounting photos across top of page on torn patterned paper. Mount remaining photo over mesh paper (Magic Mesh). Accent with vellum journaling strip and additional jewel shapes.

Mary-Catherine Kropinski, Maple Ridge, British Columbia, Canada

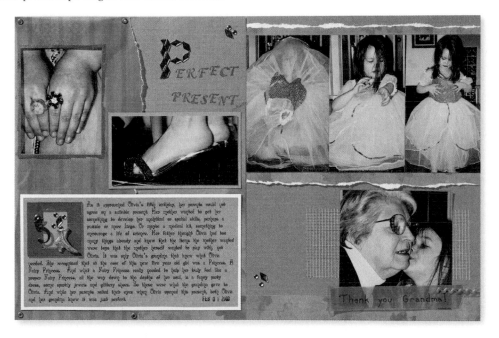

Maasai the Princess

Maria combined coordinating patterned papers and page accents to echo the attitude and clothing of her daughter's diva-esque dress-up poses. Mat sections from purple and pink striped papers (American Crafts) to white cardstock to form two halves. Tear rectangle sections from purple and pink solid papers and adhere to coordinating half of page. Layer with photos matted on white cardstock. Leave cropped photo unmatted and cover with purple vellum; adhere to center of page. Partially tuck journaled tag (Brindy's Giftables) behind photo. Embellish page with square-punched vellum decorated with stickers (Frances Meyer). Complete by affixing pink and purple fibers along top of page.

Maria Newport, Smyrna, Georgia

Alexandra, 9

Blossom

Polly artfully combines several page accents to create a feminine, well-balanced design. Affix pink satin ribbon (Offray) across each floral-patterned paper (Daisy D's) background page. Mat photos on pale pink, striped or polka-dot patterned papers (Lasting Impressions); tear bottom edge of photo mats for right page. Accent photos and photo mats with ribbon (Offray), vellum flower tag (Making Memories), handwritten tag (Avery), brads, flower (All Night Media) and leaf punches (Family Treasures) and pink button. Mount all photos to pages. Accent left page with metal-rimmed tags (Making Memories) layered with gingham-patterned paper (Frances Meyer). Journal; mount one tag atop punched leaves in upper left corner. "Hang" other journaling tag from photo on beaded chain. Create flower embellishment from metal rimmed tag, gingham paper and pink satin ribbon; adhere over punched leaves in upper right corner. Use die-cut letters (QuicKutz) to form title from two shades of pink paper. Use template (Frances Meyer) and pink cardstock to create envelope accent on right page; decorate with vellum flower tag (Making Memories), flower punch, button and chalk. Enclose handwritten journaling on patterned paper (Lasting Impressions) accented with ribbon.

Polly McMillan, Bullhead City, Arizona

Lauren's Pal

Cheerful colors and flower accents add a great deal of charm to this page dedicated to girlfriends. Layer yellow patterned paper backgrounds (Lasting Impressions) with sections of blue dot paper (Creative Imaginations). For left page, mat photo on white cardstock adorned with border stickers (Creative Imaginations), then to scalloped-edge yellow cardstock mat created with decorative scissors. Adhere to blue dot patterned paper (Lasting Impressions); chalk sides with blue chalk and mount to torn yellow dot patterned paper (Lasting Impressions) with foam adhesive. Adhere to background page. Handwrite on rectangle accent tags (Making Memories) with black pen; chalk. Embellish circle tag (Making Memories) with chalked flower punch (EK Success). Construct title using letter templates (EK Success); adorn with buttons and additional punched flowers. For right page, mat photos on white cardstock and adhere. Layer rectangle tags with patterned papers (Lasting Impressions); journal and mount. Handwrite additional journaling on vellum, adhere over blue patterned paper and accent with floral die cuts (Renae Lindgren). Enclose flower patch (Patch It) and small rectangle tag in a sheer pouch (Country Home Collections); affix to lower right corner. To complete, create borders for both pages using ribbon and border stickers (Creative Imaginations).

Polly McMillan, Bullhead City, Arizona

Little Ladies Who Lunch

Andrea used whimsical colors and accents to contribute to the mood of her daughter's first official tea party. Tear edges of patterned paper (Provo Craft) and mount on purple cardstock. Single, double and triple mat photos on various colors of cardstock; adhere to pages. For left page, embellish rectangle tags (Making Memories) by coloring with colored pencils and layering with stickers (Printworks); finish with paper yarn (Making Memories). Create title by layering letter stickers (Colorbök, Provo Craft, Creative Imaginations, C-Thru-Ruler) on patterned paper (Provo Craft) framed with pink cardstock. Adorn with curled wire, flower eyelets (source unknown), circle tag (Making Memories) and flower button (source unknown). Embellish both pages with journaling printed on green cardstock cut into graphic shapes.

Andrea Miller, The Woodlands, Texas

It Is Hard Work Being Beautiful

After serving as Mommy's photo shoot models, these two glamour girls decided they'd had enough. Kate features this very last photo opportunity with complementary colored papers and fibers. Triple mat photo on white cardstock and patterned paper (Colors By Design). Adhere to textured background cardstock (Bazzill). Print title and journaling on white cardstock with colored ink. Mat on blue cardstock and adhere to background; accent with square shapes cut from patterned paper and sun-shaped nailheads (source unknown). Complete by creating fiber border across top of journaling block; attach to center of page with nailhead and adhere ends to back of page.

Kate Nelson, Fountain, Colorado

Ladies Night

Heidi recorded an evening devoted exclusively to all-girl activities on bright and whimsical paper adorned with fun accents. Mount pictures on patterned paper (Pixie Press) and embellish with three-dimensional stickers (Westrim). Print journaling on green and yellow vellum. Create title with letter stickers (Creative Imaginations).

Heidi Bishop, Rockford, Illinois

Girlfriends

Several layered strips and fibers create a dimensional and eye-appealing page. Tear section from solid pink paper and layer horizontally across pink dot background paper (Paper Fever). Journal on vellum; leave room for metal title accent (Making Memories). Embellish with fibers and metal flower (Making Memories) and adhere to torn pink strip. Create border along left side of page by layering torn strip of pink patterned paper (Paper Fever) on torn purple cardstock. Embellish with fibers strung through cropped photos inside metal-rimmed tags (Making Memories). Accent with metal charms (Making Memories). Offset photo mounted on torn patterned papers (Paper Fever) and pink and purple cardstocks. Adorn with metal flower (Making Memories) attached by pink brad.

Heather Uppencamp, Provo, Utah

Sing Giggle Play Dance

Trudy combined texture and soft colors to create an eclectic and well-balanced design. Tear edges of vertically striped patterned paper (Sandylion) and adhere to yellow cardstock. Tear edges of horizontally striped paper (Sandylion); adhere to layout and machine stitch on opposite sides. Print journaling on transparency; adhere to page with spray adhesive. Double mat photo on shades of yellow cardstock; mount on page. Create title using metal words (Making Memories). String fibers through charms, jump rings, beads and vellum tags (Making Memories). Decorate tags with flower sticker (EK Success) and stamped words (Hero Arts). Finish with wire dragonfly (Westrim). Accent with eyelet quote (Making Memories).

Trudy Sigurdson, Victoria, British Columbia, Canada

*Haley, 7
and
Dakota*

TRAVELING IN A PACK

DRAMA QUEENS

TALKING A MILLION MILES AN HOUR

SINGING THE THEME SONG FROM "BLUE'S CLUES"

GIGGLING ABOUT EVERY LITTLE THING

HELPING US CELEBRATE MAYSIE'S 12TH BIRTHDAY

FRIENDSHIPS FORGED TO LAST A LIFETIME

MAY 9, 2003

Sweet Girls

A monochromatic backdrop allows photos and accents to become the focus of Mellette's eye-pleasing design. For left page, machine stitch pale yellow cardstock panel to mustard-colored cardstock background. Mount focal photo on white cardstock. Attach charms (Hirschberg Schutz & Co.) to eyelets in photo mat using jump rings; adhere to page with foam adhesive. Embellish with photos mounted on patterned premade accents (KI Memories). Handwrite names under photos with black pen. Finish page by crisscrossing green ribbon (Offray) across page; affix ends to back of page. Accent with plastic watch glass (Deluxe Plastic Arts) layered over premade embellishment (KI Memories) where ribbons intersect. For right page, print journaling on pale yellow cardstock; embellish with premade accent. Mount photos to background cardstock. Wrap pale yellow cardstock block with green ribbon and flower charms hanging from jump rings; machine stitch journaling block and ribbon-wrapped accent to page; add watch glass and premade embellishment to center of page to complete.

Mellette Berezoski, Crosby, Texas

First Haircut

Debbie treated patterned papers with several aging techniques, adding vintage charm to her design documenting her daughter's first haircut. Age purple patterned paper background pages (Chatterbox) by lightly rubbing with sandpaper. For left page, sand and crumple striped patterned paper (Chatterbox) for vertical border; flatten and adhere. Mount umatted photos along striped border and accent with flower eyelet (Making Memories). Sand, tear, crumple and chalk striped paper section; layer with crumpled floral paper and picture framed with metal photo corners (Making Memories). Print journaling on pink patterned paper (Chatterbox). Age paper by sanding, tearing and inking. Create page title with letter stamps (PSX Design). Mount to background. For right page, repeat paper-aging techniques for striped border, photo mat and journaling block. Accent page with additional flower eyelets, haircut certificate and plastic envelope containing lock of hair.

Debbie Kuehl, Green Bay, Wisconsin

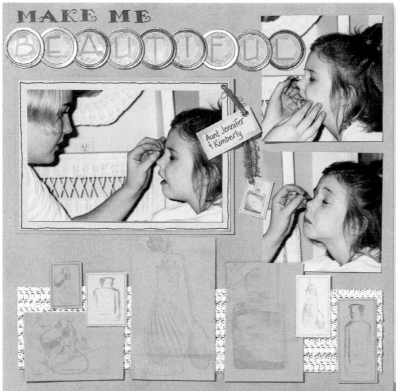

Make Me Beautiful

Brooke utilized perfume bottle accents to enhance a fun-with-make-up moment. Begin with pink cardstock background pages. For each page, layer strips of white rubber shelf liner with various perfume bottle accents (Club Scrap). Double mat each page's focal photo on purple and green cardstocks; add purple pen detail. Hang tags created with paper images (Club Scrap) from photo corners with fibers. Adhere remaining unmatted photos to pages. Construct title for left page by using lettering templates (Crafter's Workshop) and a purple pen for "Make Me." Layer letter stickers (Club Scrap) on metal-rimmed tags (Office Max) for "Beautiful." To complete, journal directly onto right page with purple pen.

Brooke Sparks, Louisville, Kentucky

Tea Party

Lisa created an original accent by scanning the saucer from her daughter's tea set and printing it onto vellum. Layer sections of flower-patterned paper (Colorbök) on pink cardstock background pages. Create title by printing in light gray ink onto cream-colored cardstock. Immediately after printing, sprinkle with glitter embossing powder (Ranger) and heat to set; mat on dark pink cardstock and embellish with tea set clip art and flower stickers (EK Success). Scan and print image of saucer on vellum to use as an accent. Mount photo, layering over accent. For right page, print journaling on pink vellum. Tear vellum and adhere to page. Accent journaling block with beads (Blue Moon Beads) strung on wire. Mount photos. Embellish page with additional flower stickers.

Lisa Francis, New Castle, Indiana

Rachel, 9

Baby Love

Ursula features a precious photo of an unsuspecting young "mommy" and her baby with soft colors and patterned papers. For left page, layer patterned paper (Colorbök) and pink textured cardstock (Bazzill) and mount vertically on teal background, covering half of page. Layer patterned paper and pink cardstock over torn vellum strip; chalk edges of vellum with pink chalk and mount vertically across page. Print title and clip art on yellow textured cardstock; adhere over paper and vellum strips. Mount photo on pink cardstock cut with decorative scissors; detail using a hole punch. Accent page with swirl clips and flower clip art embossed with clear powder mounted on foam adhesive. For right page, adhere photos along top of page. Affix patterned paper strip along bottom. Print journaling on yellow textured cardstock; accent with heart poem stone (Creative Imaginations) and swirl clip. Embellish circle tags (Making Memories) with paper, punched shapes and letter stickers (Provo Craft); hang from additional embossed clip art flowers.

Ursula Page, Virginia Beach, Virginia
Photos: Kristina Lee, Alpine, Utah

Twilight in the Tropics

Ashley incorporated several photos in her layout, as well as the vibrant pink of her dress in her choice of paper color. Begin with bold pink cardstock background pages. Dog ear opposite corners of cardstock and secure small squares of white paper with white eyelets behind. Mat two photos on white paper and adhere to each page. Mount all remaining photos. Hang tag (DMD) from one corner with handwritten date in black ink. Print journaling and title on vellum and adhere. Create bottom border on each page with a single strand of fiber.

Ashley Hamman, Peru, Indiana
Photos: Douglas Studios, Kokomo, Indiana

Princess

Janice created a unique computer-generated design for her daughter's eighth-grade graduation. Create a special-effects background using brushes to give a textured appearance (Adobe Photoshop 7.0). Form another background using distressed stars created from brushes; span across width of page. Create star frame using defined shapes overlaid on frame image; apply metallic effects using Eye Candy 4000 Chrome filter. Create frame, fill with color and texture to resemble leather. Use preset shapes to define tag, layer and add stitching. Add glamorous effects to photos by removing the subject, blurring the background, and replacing the subject as a new layer. To re-create this layout manually, layer patterned papers on background and attach with brads. Frame photo with punched shapes and embellish with shaker tag.

Janice Dye-Szucs, Oshawa, Ontario, Canada

Cover Girls

Peggy created her graphic layout using clean and simple lines with bold colors. Mount photos to black cardstock. Print journaling on white cardstock; mount on red cardstock. Repeat for small section at top left corner of page. To create title, print mirror image on red cardstock; cut with a craft knife and adhere.

Peggy Roarty, Council Bluffs, Iowa

Look Who's Driving!

Victoria created car key accents and a journaling tag to mimic a key chain on this new-driver page. Tear blue cardstock along one side and mount to speckled tan paper background. Mat two photos on blue cardstock; adhere to bottom half of page. Create tag accent by printing title and journaling on tan paper. Cut into tag shape and tear bottom edge; mount on blue cardstock. Handcut key accents from metallic paper; string through metal key ring and tag accent; mount to page.

Victoria Jimenez, Harrah, Oklahoma

The Mere Chink of Cups and Saucers...

Michaela's choice of feminine floral accents adds extra elegance to her daughter's tiny tea party. Begin with periwinkle textured cardstock background pages (Bazzill). For left page, layer focal photo on white mulberry paper and blue cardstock. Accent corner with flower stickers (source unknown). Mat secondary photos on blue cardstock and adhere to page. Print title on vellum. Tear and chalk edges with blue chalk; attach to blue cardstock with silver brads. Mount to page. Create tag accents by layering tags (Making Memories) with additional flower stickers and stamping words with letter stamps (PSX Design). Highlight words with blue chalk. Finish tags with blue eyelet and sheer blue ribbon (Offray). For right page, print journaling onto vellum. Tear both sides, chalk edges and layer over block of blue cardstock. Mount strip to background. Affix two photos to blue cardstock. Accent one end with mulberry paper and small tags adorned with flower stickers and ribbon. Mount to top of page. Mount remaining photo and additional tag to complete.

Michaela Young-Mitchell, Morenci, Arizona

Summer Dresses

Tarri showcased several pictures of her daughter's summer dresses and created accents that mirror the details in her shoes. Adhere floral patterned paper (Paper Patch) to pink cardstock background pages. Mat photos on sections of yellow and blue cardstocks; adhere to pages over floral patterned paper. For journaling tags, print on pink cardstock and cut into small tag shapes. Accent with flower punches (EK Success) and silver brads; finish with embroidery floss. Place tags in vellum envelopes (Card Connection) and adhere along bottom of pages beneath photos. Create title by printing mirror image on blue and yellow cardstocks; cut out with craft knife. Embellish both pages with additional flower punches, brads and two photos matted on blue and yellow cardstocks; affix all to pages.

Tarri Botwinski, Grand Rapids, Michigan

Little Sleeping Beauty

Subtle floral patterned paper and dreamy accents add to the fairy tale charm of Oksanna's design, which features her daughter in her wedding dress and veil. For left page, print journaling on patterned paper background (Design Originals). Tear bottom edge of vellum and adhere to page with spray adhesive. Set three eyelets in photo; "hang" patterned paper tags (Design Originals) created using template (Accu-Cut) from fibers. Mount on tan cardstock mat and adhere to vellum. Embellish tags with title created from cardstock strips and letter stamps (All Night Media). For right page, mat tan cardstock on cream cardstock; layer with patterned paper strip and spray with glitter (Duncan). Adhere photos. Create tag accent using template (Accu-Cut); layer with patterned paper and machine stitch border around edge. Layer with title created from cardstock strips and letter stamps; finish with fibers. Accent with heart punch (EK Success) embellished with dimensional paint (Duncan).

Oksanna Pope, Los Gatos, California

Girls

Brandi chose colors that blend well with her sepia-toned photos and used accents to add dimensional flare. Begin with patterned paper background (Deluxe Designs). Stamp texture using watermark ink (Tsukineko) and rubber stamp (Raindrops On Roses) on plum-colored paper; mount to background page. Mount picture frame (Leeco) with foam adhesive over focal photo. Embellish frame with rose accents (Leeco). Create title with metal letters (Making Memories). Layer rose tags (Leeco) with vellum tags (Making Memories) finished with metal eyelet accents (Making Memories).

Brandi Ginn, Lafayette, Colorado

Playing Dress-Up At Grandma's

Only clean lines and minimal accents were needed to dress up this charming dress-up page. Frame textured pink cardstock (Bazzill) on black cardstock. Use metal corners (Making Memories) to accent. Accent with gingham ribbon (JoAnn Fabrics). Mat photos on black cardstock and adhere to page. Print journaling on pale pink textured cardstock (Bazzill); accent with metal plaque (Making Memories). Mat journaling block on black cardstock and adhere to page. Create title with letter stickers (Wordsworth, SEI).

Tracy Miller, Fallston, Maryland

A Smile As Sweet As Spring

Kelli created an intricate page border by utilizing numerous punches, papers and colorful beads. Mount blue cardstock to textured purple cardstock (Bazzill). Adhere strip of green velveteen paper (Wintech) along bottom; layer with fence border (source unknown). Chalk fence for dimension. Create punch art flowers with various punches (EK Success, Emagination Crafts, Punch Bunch) and colored papers. Double mat photo on pink and purple cardstocks. Create photo corners using wire and beads. Print part of title on pink cardstock with purple ink. Cut into tag shapes. Use metal letters (Making Memories) for remaining words. Mount title on yellow dot paper (Doodlebug Design) and pink and purple cardstocks. Embellish with buttons. Print journaling on yellow dot paper; mat on pink paper and accent with green triangles adorned with buttons. Mount on flip book created from textured purple cardstock that conceals additional photos inside.

Kelli Gamble, Austintown, Ohio

My Hair

Kim records her various hairstyles from over the years, making for a fun and memorable layout. For left page, print journaling on blue cardstock. Mat photo on black cardstock and adhere to textured burgundy cardstock (Bazzill). Print title on vellum; attach to layout with oversized brads (Making Memories). Embellish slide mount with patterned vellum (SEI) and circle accent (KI Memories). Create border title with letter stickers (Creative Imaginations) and accent with patterned vellum. For right page, square-crop photos in various sizes; mat on black cardstock and adhere in three rows across page. Adhere patterned vellum strip along bottoms of photos.

Kim Haynes, Harrah, Oklahoma

Hailee, 4

Diva Darlings

Here a special friendship is defined with a unique photo mat highlighted with sticker words. Mat patterned paper (Chatterbox) on black cardstock. Tear strip of patterned paper (Paper Adventures) and adhere along left side of page. Triple mat photo on black and white cardstocks, leaving room for word stickers (Creative Imaginations). Print journaling on white paper; mat on torn patterned paper (Paper Adventures). Age flower stickers (Paper House Productions) with sandpaper and mount on black cardstock. Layer large aged flower on corrugated cardstock; add yellow circle and thread with gingham ribbon. Attach mini calendar page (Impress Rubber Stamps) with black nailheads (Chatterbox).

Linda Beeson, Ventura, California

Shopathon

Kristin incorporated clothing designer tags into her layout to use as fun accents and also for evidence of a successful shopping trip! Print journaling on textured blue cardstock (Bazzill) and logo clip art. Mount denim frame (My Mind's Eye) over photo, and denim pocket (My Mind's Eye) over fashion labels. Mount pocket with eyelets. Create title using letter punches (EK Success) on denim strip; adhere with eyelets. Accent page with additional eyelets strung with fiber.

Kristin Cleary, Wallingford, Connecticut

Page Title Ideas

At a loss for a too-perfect-for-words page title? Remedy your "writer's block" by utilizing the lists of sample sentiments below for creative inspiration. You can custom-coordinate your page titles with handmade or computer-generated designs. For additional artistic flare, accent page titles with embellishments that speak to your pictures and provide added punch to your page theme.

Sugar and...

All girl
All you need to be is you
Always remember to be happy
Angel among us
Angel face
Beautiful you
Beauty comes from within
Beauty in bloom
Butterfly kisses
Cute as a button
Cutie pie
Daddy's girl
Darling daughter
Earth angel
A girl is..
Girl next door
Girly girl
Isn't she lovely?
Little girls, like butterflies, need no excuse
Little lady
Little princess
Mommy's angel
Mommy's helper
More sugar than spice
My girl
Picture perfect
Portrait of a lady
Precious little one
Pretty as a picture
Pretty in pink
Pretty is as pretty does
Simply sweet
Sitting pretty
Sleeping beauty
Sweetheart
Sweet innocence
Sweet slumber
Sweet stuff
Thank heaven for little girls
There was a little girl
Tickled pink
Too sweet for words
What is a girl?
You can't hide beautiful
You make life sweet
100% girl

Spice!

All girl...almost
All grrrl
Angel with an attitude

Attitude is everything
A girl's gotta do what a girl's gotta do
Beauty and the beast
Been there, done that
Big girls do cry
Daredevil
Diva
Diva in training
Diva moment
Don't hate me because I'm beautiful
Drama queen
Free spirit
Funny girl
Gender bender
Gigglebox
Girl power
Girls rule
Girls rule, boys drool
I am woman, hear me roar!
I have an attitude and I know how to use it
It's all about the attitude
Little miss cool
Little women
More spice than sugar
Sassy
Semi-precious
She's all that
She's got personality
Spirited
Spunky
Starlet
Talk to the hand
Teen queen
Tell it like it is
That's my girl!
T'ween queen
Uptown girl
Wild angel
Wild child
Wild one
Wild thing, you make my heart sing
Woman-child

Girls Just Wanna Have Fun

All girl all-star
And away she goes!
Atta girl!
Backyard beauty
Ballerina girl

Bathing beauty
Champion
Coming into her own
Dancing queen
Dare to dream
Don't be afraid to soar
Dream big
Girl meets world
Girl on the go
Girl wonder
Girls can do anything boys can do
Girls just wanna have fun
Going places
It is a happy talent to know how to play
A little dirt never hurt
Nature girl
She's not just a pretty face
Shoot for the stars
Silly girl
Skater girl
The sky's the limit
Surfer girl
Sweet victory
Tiny dancer
Watch out world
When I see you smile
Working girl
Yes, girls can!
You are my shining star
You glow girl
You go girl

It's a Girl Thing

All dolled up
All dressed up and no place to go
Baby love
Bad hair day
Boys, boys, boys
Clothes don't make the girl
Cover girl
Feeling fancy
Girlfriends
Girlfriends forever
Girl-isms
Girl talk
Girls' night out
Girls only
Glamour girl
I enjoy being a girl
I feel pretty
It's a girl's world
It's not easy being beautiful

Just girls being girls
Ladies night
Lady fingers
Like mother, like daughter
Makeover madness
Material girl
Modern woman

No boys allowed
Petticoat junction
Putting on the glitz
She's got the look
Shopping spree
Sisterhood
Sleepover

Slumber party
Social butterfly
Spa treatment
Strike a pose
Supermodel
Tea for two
What a doll

Additional Instructions & Credits

Cover

Enlarge definition page from dictionary (Merriam-Webster) using photocopy machine; tear along top and bottom edge. Mount on textured cardstock (Bazzill); highlight definition with green vellum. Mount picture on textured cardstock (Bazzill) and tear bottom edge. Use jump rings (Westrim) to attach beads (Halcraft). Stamp letters (Just For Fun) on green vellum using solvent-based ink (Tsukineko); accent with pressed flower (Nature's Pressed). Place sheets of mica (USArtQuest) atop vellum. Attach with eyelets, clasp (Westrim) and ribbon (Offray).

Jodi Amidei, Memory Makers Photos: Ken Trujillo, Memory Makers Inspired by Betsy Sammarco, New Canaan, Connecticut

Page 1 Six Reasons It's Great to Be a Girl

Begin with a textured green cardstock background (Bazzill). Cut a strip and large block of floral embossed vellum (K & Company); layer strip along right edge of page and block to left side of page. Print journaling on pink paper. Accent with green buttons (Making Memories) tied with embroidery floss (Making Memories). Mount journaling along right edge over vellum strip. Print mirror image of title on pink paper and cut out with craft knife. Mount photo on pink paper and adhere at a slight angle.

Michele Woods, Worthington, Ohio

Page 3 Bookplate

Cut tag shape from white glossy paper (Ranger) using a template (C-Thru Ruler). Create patterned background with stamp (EK Success) and embossing ink. Heat emboss with clear embossing powder. Use finger dauber to rub pink ink into tag. Mark leaf patterns using template (Timeless Touches); stitch with embroidery floss (Timeless Touches) and color leaves with green ink. Complete by inking edges of tag with green ink and adding ribbon (Making Memories), button and charm (Jesse James) embellishments.

Jodi Amidei, Memory Makers

Page 6 Anna and Sasha

Mat floral patterned paper (K & Company) on green cardstock background. Using craft knife, cut flower from additional sheet of patterned paper and coordinating patterned vellum (K & Company). Mount cut vellum to cut flowers; adhere over pattern in background paper using foam adhesive for dimension. Triple mat focal photo on green and floral patterned papers; treat edges with green metallic rub-ons (Craft-T) and ink. Affix to page. Cut strip from coordinating patterned paper (K & Company); adhere pink ribbon to each side. Mat photos on green cardstock and embellish with vellum-layered patterned paper accent. Adhere strip to left side of page. For journaling block, print journaling on pink cardstock. Treat edges of pink and green cardstocks with green and pink metallic run-ons and inks; adhere green photo corners to pink cardstock and mat on green cardstock. Create names using die cuts (QuicKutz); adorn with rhinestones (Me & My Big Ideas). Mount journaling block to page.

Photos: Ken Trujillo, Memory Makers

Page 7 Tea Time

Treat textured burgundy cardstock background (Bazzill) by very lightly applying cream-colored paint (Delta) with a stiff-bristled paintbrush. Cut three strips of striped patterned paper (Making Memories) and tear three strips from patterned papers (Anna Griffin). Mount two strips of striped paper to bottom half of page and one along left side of page; layer each with torn patterned paper strip, weaving patterned papers where they intersect. Embellish each with green ribbon (Fiber Scraps). Create tag accents by stamping patterned paper with letter stamps (Stampendous) and layering with clear plastic tags (K & Company); trim patterned paper to fit tag, stamp edges of tag with burgundy inkpad and embellish with green ribbon. Adhere tags along paper border and embellish with buttons (EK Success). Double mat photos on burgundy textured cardstock and patterned papers; mount to page; adorning focal photo with tag and green ribbon. For journaling block, print journaling onto a transparency. When dry, very lightly apply cream-colored paint with a stiff bristled brush on back; further treat with burgundy inkpad. Embellish with tea set accents (EK Success).

Jodi Amidei, Memory Makers Books Photos: Michele Gerbrandt, Memory Makers

Artist
Index

Sources

The following companies manufacture workspace and storage products featured in this book. Please check your local retailers to find these materials, or go to a company's Web site for the latest product. In addition, we have made every attempt to properly credit the items mentioned in this book. We apologize to any company that we have listed incorrectly, and we would appreciate hearing from you.

3L Corp.
(800) 828-3130
www.3lcorp.com

3M Stationary
(800) 364-3577
www.3m.com

7 Gypsies
(480) 325-3358
www.7gypsies.com

ACCO Brands, Inc.
www.acco.com

Adobe
www.adobe.com

Accu-Cut® (wholesale only)
(800) 288-1670
www.accucut.com

All My Memories
(888) 553-1998
www.allmymemories.com

All Night Media (see Plaid Enterprises)

All The Extras
www.alltheextras.com

Alphabet Soup- no contact info. available

American Art Clay Co. (AMACO)
(800) 374-1600
www.amaco.com

American Crafts (wholesale only)
(8000) 879-5185
www.americancrafts.com

American Tag Company
(800) 223-3956
www.americantag.net

Amscan, Inc.
(800) 444-8887
www.amscan.com

Anna Griffin, Inc. (wholesale only)
(888) 817-8170
www.annagriffin.co

ANW Crestwood Papers
www.anwcrestwood.com

Artistic Expressions
(219) 763-1356
www.artisticexpressionsincdel.com

Artistic Scrapper
(818) 786-8304
www.artisticscrapper.com

Artistic Wire Ltd.™
(630) 530-7567
www.artisticwire.com

Autumn Leaves (wholesale only)
(800) 588-6707
www.autumnleaves.com

Avery
(800) GO-AVERY
www.avery.com

Bazzill Basics Paper
(480) 558-8557
www.bazzillbasics.com

Beary Patch Inc., The (wholesale only)
(403) 626-3600
www.bearypatchinc.com

BEHR Process Corporation
(714) 545-7101
www.behr.com

Blue Moon Beads
(800) 377-6715
www.beads.net

Bo-Bunny Press
(801) 771-0481
www.bobunny.com

Boutique Trims, Inc.
(248) 437-2017
www.boutiquetrims.com

Boxer Scrapbook Productions
(888) 625-6255
www.boxerscrapbooks.com

Brindy's Giftables
www.brindysgiftables.com

Broderbund
www.broderbund.com

Brown Bag Fibers
www.brownbagfibers.com

Buttons Gallore
(856) 753-6700
www.buttonsgaloreandmore.com

Card Connection, The
(see Michaels Arts & Crafts)

CARL Mfg. USA, Inc. (wholesale only)
(800) 257-4771
www.Carl-Products.com

Carolee's Creations®
(435) 563-1100
www.carolees.com

Charming Place, A
(509) 325-5655
www.acharmingplace.com

Charming Spirits- no contact info available

Chatterbox, Inc.
(208) 939-9133
www.chatterboxinc.com

Cherished Memories- no contact info avaialble

Chronicle Books
www.chroniclebooks.com

Clearsnap®, Inc. (wholesale only)
(800) 448-4862
www.clearsnap.com

Close To My Heart®
(888) 655-6552
www.closetomyheart.com

Club Scrap™, Inc.
(888) 634-9100
www.clubscrap.com

Collections- no contact info available

Colorbök™, Inc. (wholesale only)
(800) 366-4660
www.colorbok.com

Colors By Design
(800) 832-8436
www.colorsbydesign.com

Country Home Collections- no contact info available

Crafter's Workshop, The
(877) CRAFTER
www.thecraftersworkshop.com

Craft-T Products
(507) 235-3996
www.craf-tproducts.com

Crafts, Etc.
www.craftsetc.com

Creative Imaginations (wholesale only)
(800) 942-6487
www.cigift.com

Creative Impressions
(719) 596-4860
www.creativeimpressions.com

Creative Memories®
(800) 468-9335
www.creativememories.com

Cross-My-Heart-Cards, Inc. (Scrapbook Collection) (wholesale only)
(888) 689-8808
www.crossmyheart.com

C-Thru® Ruler Company, The (wholesale only)
(800) 243-8419
www.cthruruler.com

Cut-It-Up™
(530) 389-2233
www.cut-it-up.com

Daisy D's Paper Company
(888) 601-8955
www.daisydspaper.com

Delta Technical Coatings, Inc.
(800) 423-4135
www.deltacrafts.com

Deluxe Designs
(480) 497-9005
www.deluxecuts.com

Deluxe Plastic Arts- no contact info available

Dena Designs
www.denadesigns.com

Design Originals
(800) 877-7820
www.designoriginals.com

DieCuts with a View™
(801) 224-6766
www.diecutswithaview.com
DMC Corp.
(973) 589-0606
www.dmc-usa.com
DMD Industries, Inc.
(wholesale only)
(800) 805-9890
www.dmdind.com
Doodlebug Design Inc.™
(801) 966-9952
Duncan Enterprises
(559) 294-3282
www.duncan-enterprises.com
Dymo
(800) 426-7827
www.dymo.com
Eastman Kodak
www.kodak.com
EK Success™, Ltd. (wholesale only)
(800) 524-1349
www.eksuccess.com
Emagination Crafts, Inc.
(wholesale only)
(630) 833-9521
www.emaginationcrafts.com
Embelleez Retail
(516) 510-3286
www.embelleez.com
Eyelets, Etc.
(303) 921-0476
www.eyelets-etc.com
Family Treasures, Inc.®
www.familytreasures.com
Fibers By The Yard
(800) 760-8901
www.fibersbytheyard.com
Fiber Scraps
(215) 230-4905
www.fiberscraps.com
Fiskars, Inc. (wholesale only)
(715) 842-2091
www.fiskars.com
FoofaLa
(402) 330-3208
www.foofala.com
Frances Meyer, Inc.
(800) 372-6237
www.francesmeyer.com
Funky Fibers
www.funkyfibers.com
Great Canadian Stamp Company
Graphic Products Corporation
(800) 323-1660
www.gpcpapers.com
Halcraft USA, Inc.
(212) 367-1580
www.halcraft.com
Hero Arts® Rubber Stamps, Inc.
(wholesale only)
(800) 822-4376
www.heroarts.com
Hillcreek Designs
(619) 562-5799
www.hillcreekdesigns.com
Hirschberg Schutz & Co.
(wholesale only)
(800) 221-8640
Hobby Lobby
www.hobbylobby.com
Hot Off the Press, Inc.
(800) 227-9595
www.paperpizazz.com
Hyglo®/American Pin Fastener
(wholesale only)
(800) 821-7125
www.american-pin.com
Impress Rubber Stamps
(206) 901-9101
www.impressrubberstamps.com
Impression Obsession Stamps
www.impression-obsession.com
Inkadinkado® Rubber Stamps
(800) 888-4652
www.inkadinkado.com

It Takes Two®
(800) 331-9843
www.ittakestwo.com
Ivy Cottage Creations
www.ivycottagecreations.com
Jacquard Products
(707) 433-9577
www.jacquardproducts.com
Jennifer Collection, The
(518) 272-4572
Jesse James and Co., Inc.
(610) 435-0201
www.jessejamesbutton.com
Jest Charming
(702) 564-5101
www.jestcharming.com
JewelCraft, LLC
(201) 223-0804
www.jewelcraft.biz
Jim Stephan
(760) 373-8896
www.jimstephan.net
JoAnn Fabrics
www.joann.com
Just For Fun®
(727) 938-9898
www.jffstamps.com
K & Company
(888) 244-2083
www.kandcompany.com
Kangaroo and Joey
(480) 460-4841
www.kangarooandjoey.com
Karen Foster Design™
(wholesale only)
(801) 451-9779
www.karenfosterdesign.com
Keeping Memories Alive™
(800) 419-4949
www.scrapbooks.com
KI Memories
(469) 633-9665
www.kimemories.com
Kopp Design
(208) 656-0734
www.koppdesign.com
Lasting Impressions for Paper, Inc.
(801) 298-1979
www.lastingimpressions.com
Leapenhi Paper Designs
(250) 334-0221
www.leapenhi.com
Leeco Industries
(662) 551-1025
www.leecoindustries.com
Limited Edition Rubberstamps
(650) 594-4242
www.limitededitionrs.com
Liquitex
www.liquitex.com
Lowe's
www.lowes.com
Lucky Squirrel
(505) 861-5606
www.luckysquirrel.com
Ludwig Industries- no contact info available
Magenta Rubber Stamps
(wholesale only)
(800) 565-5254
www.magentarubberstamps.com
Magic Mesh™
(651) 345-6374
www.magicmesh.com
Magic Scraps™
(972) 238-1838
www.magicscraps.com
Making Memories
(800) 286-5263
www.makingmemories.com
Martha Stewart
www.marthastewart.com
Marvy® Uchida (wholesale only)
(800) 541-5877
www.uchida.com
Matchbox (see Mattel)

Mattel, Inc.
www.mattel.com
McGill, Inc.
(800) 982-9884
www.mcgillinc.com
me & my BIG ideas (wholesale only)
(949) 589-4607
www.meandmybigideas.com
Memory Crafts
www.memorycrafts.com
Merriam-Webster
www.merriam-webster.com
Michaels® Arts & Crafts
(800) 642-4235
www.michaels.com
Midnight Media- no contact info available
Mrs. Grossman's Paper Co.
(wholesale only)
(800) 429-4549
www.mrsgrossmans.com
Mustard Moon
(408) 229-8542
www.mustardmoon.com
My Mind's Eye™, Inc.
(801) 298-3709
www.frame-ups.com
Nature's Pressed
(800) 850-2499
www.naturespressed.com
NRN Designs
(800) 421-6988
www.nrndesigns.com
O' Scrap!/Imaginations!
(801) 223-6015
www.imaginations-inc.com
Office Max
www.officemax.com
Offray & Son, Inc.
www.offray.com
On The Surface
(847) 675-2520
Paper Adventures® (wholesale only)
(800) 727-0699
www.paperadventures.com
Paper Fever, Inc.
(801) 328-3560
www.paperfever.com
Paper Garden, The (wholesale only)
(702) 639-1956
www.mypapergarden.com
Paper House Productions
(800) 255-7316
www.paperhouseproductions.com
Paper Patch, The (wholesale only)
(800) 397-2737
www.paperpatch.com
Patch It- no contact info available
Pebbles, Inc. (wholesale only)
(801) 235-1520
www.pebblesinc.com
Pioneer Photo Albums, Inc.®
(800) 366-3686
www.pioneerphotoalbums.com
Pixie Press
(888) 834-2883
www.pixiepress.com
Plaid Enterprises, Inc.
(800) 842-4197
www.plaidonline.com
Polyform Products
(847) 427-0020
www.polyformproducts.com
PrintWorks
(800) 854-6558
www.printworkscollection.com
Provo Craft® (wholesale only)
(888) 577-3545
www.provocraft.com
Prym Dritz Corporation
www.dritz.com
PSX Design™
(800) 782-6748
www.psxdesign.com

Pulsar Eco Products LLC
(877) 861-0031
www.pulsarpaper.com
Punch Bunch, The
(254) 791-4209
www.thepunchbunch.com
Punch Palace
www.punchpalace.com
QuicKutz®
(888) 702-1146
www.quickutz.com
Raindrops On Roses
(307) 877-6241
www.raindropsonroses.com
Ranger Industries, Inc.
(800) 244-2211
www.rangerink.com
Robin's Nest Press, The
(wholesale only)
(435) 789-5387
www.robinsnest-scrapbook.com
Rubba Dub Dub Artist's Stamps
(707) 748-0929
www.artsanctum.com
Sakura of America
(800) 776-6257
www.gellyroll.com
Sanford
www.sanfordcorp.com
Sandylion Sticker Designs
(wholesale only)
(800) 387-4215
www.sandylion.com
Sarah Lugg
www.sarahlugg.com
ScrapArts
(503) 631-4893
www.scraparts.com
Scrap Pagerz™
(435) 645-0696
www.scrappagerz.com
Scrapbook Mania
(318) 868-0909
Scrappin' Sports & More
(419) 225-9751
www.scrappinsports.com
Scrap-Ease® (What's New LTD)
(wholesale only)
(800) 272-3874
www.whatsnewltd.com
Scrapyard 329
(775) 829-1118
www.scrapyard329.com
SEI, Inc.
(800) 333-3279
www.shopsei.com
Sizzix
(866) 742-4447
www.sizzix.com
Solum World
(505) 255-3534
Stampcraft (see Plaid Enterprises)
Stamp Doctor, The
(208) 342-4362
www.stampdoctor.com
Stampa Rosa- no longer in business
Stampendous!®
(800) 869-0474
www.stampendous.com
Stamp In The Hand Co., A
(wholesale only)
(310) 884-9700
www.astampinthehand.com
Stampin' Up!®
(800) 782-6787
www.stampinup.com
Sticker Studio, The
(208) 322-2465
www.stickerstudio.com
Streamline-no contact info available
Sulyn Industries, Inc.
www.sulyn.com
Suze Weinberg Design Studio
(732) 761-2400
www.schmoozewithsuze.com

Target
www.target.com
Timeless Images- no contact info available
Timeless Touches
(623) 362-8285
www.timelesstouches.net
Treehouse Designs
(877) 372-1109
www.treehouse-designs.com
Tsukineko®, Inc.
(800) 769-6633
www.tsukineko.com
Two Peas In A Bucket
www.twopeasinabucket.com
Uptown Design Company™
(253) 925-1000
www.uptowndesign.com
USArtQuest
(800) 200-7848
www.usartquest.com
Wallies
www.wallies.com
Wal-Mart
www.walmart.com
Westrim® Crafts
(800) 727-2727
www.westrim.com
Wichelt Imports, Inc.
www.wichelt.com
Wintech International Corp.
(800) 263-6043
www.wintechint.com
Wordsworth Stamps
(719) 282-3495
www.wordsworthstamps.com
Yasutomo & Co.
(650) 737-8888
www.yasutomo.com

Index

Alexandra, 9